POWERNOTES

to accompany

ACCOUNTING PRINCIPLES

5th Edition

VOLUME 1 / CHAPTERS 1-13

JERRY J. WEYGANDT Ph.D., C.P.A.
Arthur Andersen Alumni Professor of Accounting
University of Wisconsin - Madison
Madison, Wisconsin

DONALD E. KIESO Ph.D., C.P.A.
KPMG Peat Marwick Emeritus Professor of Accounting
Northern Illinois University
DeKalb, Illinois

PAUL D. KIMMEL Ph.D., C.P.A.
Associate Professor of Accounting
University of Wisconsin - Milwaukee
Milwaukee, Wisconsin

Prepared By
GREGORY K. LOWRY
Mercer University

MARIANNE BRADFORD
The University of Tennessee

JOHN WILEY & SONS, INC.
New York • Chichester • Weinheim • Brisbane • Singapore • Toronto

COVER PHOTO   © Paul Souders/Tony Stone Images, New York

Table of Contents

Preface

Preface

These PowerNotes include the PowerPoint Presentation slides prepared for *Accounting Principles, Fifth Edition* by Weygandt, Kieso and Kimmel. The slides are printed out three to a page, with spaces next to each slide for you to take notes in class or on your own. The material in these PowerNotes follows the sequence of each chapter, and includes key points from the chapter and examples. This handy note-taking guide allows you to focus on the discussion at hand, instead of trying to record information projected by your instructor in the classroom.

Accounting Principles, 5e
Weygandt, Kieso, & Kimmel

Prepared by
Marianne Bradford
The University of Tennessee
Gregory K. Lowry
Macon Technical Institute

John Wiley & Sons, Inc.

CHAPTER 1
ACCOUNTING IN ACTION

After studying this chapter, you should be able to:

1 Explain the meaning of accounting.

2 Identify the users and uses of accounting.

3 Understand why ethics is a fundamental business concept.

4 Explain the meaning of generally accepted accounting principles and the cost principle.

CHAPTER 1
ACCOUNTING IN ACTION

After studying this chapter, you should be able to:

5 Explain the meaning of the monetary unit assumption and the economic entity assumption.

6 State the basic accounting equation and explain the meaning of assets, liabilities, and owner's equity.

7 Analyze the effect of business transactions on the basic accounting equation.

8 Prepare an income statement, owner's equity statement, balance sheet, and statement of cash flows.

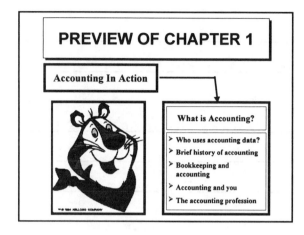

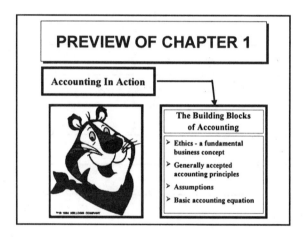

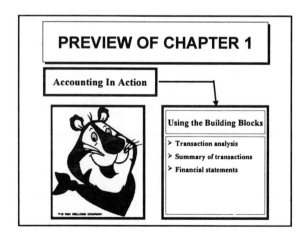

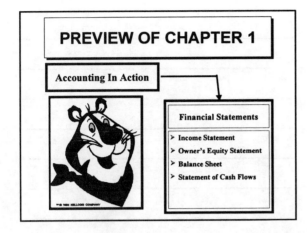

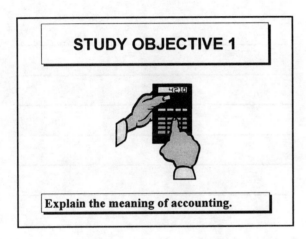

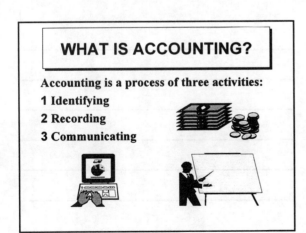

ILLUSTRATION 1-1
THE ACCOUNTING PROCESS

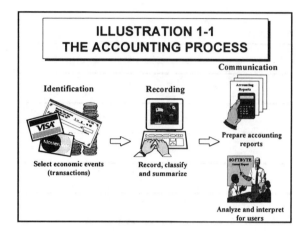

STUDY OBJECTIVE 2

Identify the users and uses and of accounting.

ILLUSTRATION 1-2
QUESTIONS ASKED BY INTERNAL USERS

Is cash sufficient to pay bills?

What is the cost of manufacturing each unit of product?

Can we afford to give employees pay raises this year?

Which product line is the most profitable?

ILLUSTRATION 1-3
QUESTIONS ASKED BY EXTERNAL USERS

Is the company earning satisfactory income?

How does the company compare in size and profitability with its competitors?

What do we do if they catch us?

Will the company be able to pay its debts as they come due?

BOOKKEEPING DISTINGUISHED FROM ACCOUNTING

Accounting

1 Includes bookkeeping

2 Also includes much more

Bookkeeping

1 Involves only the recording of economic events

2 Is just one part of accounting

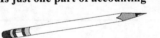

THE ACCOUNTING PROFESSION

- Public accountants offer expert service to the general public through the services they perform.
- Private accountants are employees of individual companies and are involved in a number of activities including cost and tax accounting, systems, and internal auditing.
- Not for Profit accounting includes reporting and control for government units, foundations, hospitals, labor unions, colleges/universities, and charities.

ILLUSTRATION 1-4
ACCOUNTING CAREER LADDER

Private Accounting		Public Accounting
VP Finance and CFO	10+ years	Partner
Corporate Controller	6 to 8 years	Audit Manager
Senior Accountant	2 to 4+ years	Senior Auditor
Junior Accountant	Entry level	Junior Auditor

STUDY OBJECTIVE 3

Understand why ethics is a fundamental business concept.

STUDY OBJECTIVE 4

Explain the meaning of generally accepted accounting principles and the cost principle.

STUDY OBJECTIVE 5

Explain the meaning of the monetary unit assumption and the economic entity assumption.

THE BUILDING BLOCKS OF ACCOUNTING

- Ethics - standards of conduct by which one's actions are judged as right or wrong, honest or dishonest.
- Generally Accepted Accounting Principles - primarily established by the Financial Accounting Standards Board and the Securities and Exchange Commission
- Assumptions
  1 Monetary Unit - only transaction data that can be expressed in terms of money is included in the accounting records.
  2 Economic Entity - includes any organization or unit in society.

BUSINESS ENTERPRISES

- A business owned by one person is generally a proprietorship.
- A business owned by two or more persons associated as partners is a partnership.
- A business organized as a separate legal entity under state corporation law and having ownership divided into transferable shares of stock is called a corporation.

STUDY OBJECTIVE 6

State the basic accounting equation and explain the meaning of assets, liabilities, and owner's equity.

ILLUSTRATION 1-7
BASIC ACCOUNTING EQUATION

The Basic Accounting Equation

| Assets | = | Liabilities | + | Owner's Equity |

ASSETS AS A BUILDING BLOCK

- Assets are resources owned by a business.
- They are things of value used in carrying out such activities as production and exchange.

LIABILITIES AS A BUILDING BLOCK

- Liabilities are claims against assets.
- They are existing debts and obligations.

OWNER'S EQUITY AS A BUILDING BLOCK

- Owner's Equity is equal to total assets minus total liabilities.
- Owner's Equity represents the ownership claim on total assets.
- Subdivisions of Owner's Equity:
  1 Capital
  2 Drawing
  3 Revenues
  4 Expenses

INVESTMENTS BY OWNERS AS A BUILDING BLOCK

- Investments by Owner are the assets put in the business by the owner.
- These investments in the business increase owner's equity.

DRAWINGS AS A BUILDING BLOCK

- Drawings are withdrawals of cash or other assets by the owner for personal use.
- Drawings decrease total owner's equity.

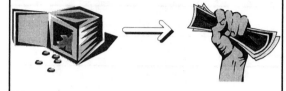

REVENUES AS A BUILDING BLOCK

- Revenues are the gross increases in owner's equity resulting from business activities entered into for the purpose of earning income.
- Revenues may result from sale or merchandise, performance of services, rental of property, or lending of money.
- Revenues usually result in an increase in an asset.

EXPENSES AS A BUILDING BLOCK

- Expenses are the decreases in owner's equity that result from operating the business.
- Expenses are the cost of assets consumed or services used in the process of earning revenue.
- Examples of expenses may be utility expense, rent expense, supplies expense, and tax expense.

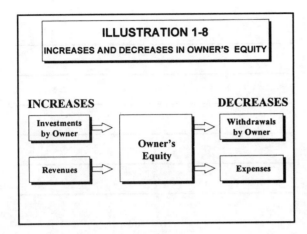

ILLUSTRATION 1-8
INCREASES AND DECREASES IN OWNER'S EQUITY

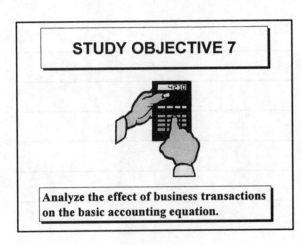

STUDY OBJECTIVE 7

Analyze the effect of business transactions on the basic accounting equation.

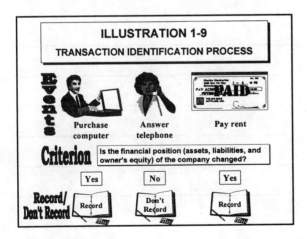

ILLUSTRATION 1-9
TRANSACTION IDENTIFICATION PROCESS

TRANSACTION ANALYSIS
TRANSACTION 1

- Ray Neal decides to open a computer programming service.
- On September 1, he invests $15,000 cash in the business, which he names Softbyte.

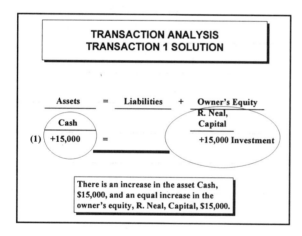

TRANSACTION ANALYSIS
TRANSACTION 1 SOLUTION

Assets	=	Liabilities	+	Owner's Equity
Cash				R. Neal, Capital
(1) +15,000	=			+15,000 Investment

There is an increase in the asset Cash, $15,000, and an equal increase in the owner's equity, R. Neal, Capital, $15,000.

TRANSACTION ANALYSIS
TRANSACTION 2

Softbyte purchases computer equipment for $7,000 cash.

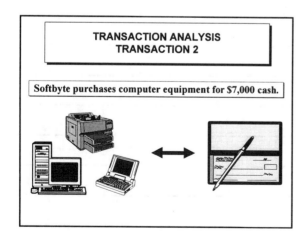

TRANSACTION ANALYSIS
TRANSACTION 2 SOLUTION

	Assets		=	Liabilities	+	Owner's Equity
						R. Neal,
	Cash	+	Equipment	=		Capital
Old Bal.	$15,000					$15,000
(2)	-7,000		+$7,000			
New Bal.	$ 8,000	+	$7,000	=		$15,000
		$15,000				

Cash is decreased $7,000, and the asset
Equipment is increased $7,000.

TRANSACTION ANALYSIS
TRANSACTION 3

- Softbyte purchases computer paper and other supplies expected to last several months from Acme Supply Company for $1,600.
- Acme Supply Company agrees to allow Softbyte to pay this bill in October, a month later.
- This transaction is often referred to as a purchase on account or a credit purchase.

TRANSACTION ANALYSIS
TRANSACTION 3 SOLUTION

	Assets				=	Liabilities	+	Owner's Equity
						Accounts		R. Neal,
	Cash	+	Supplies	+	Equipment	=	Payable	+	Capital
Old Bal.	$8,000				$7,000				$15,000
(3)			+$1,600				+$1,600		
New Bal.	$8,000	+	$1,600	+	$7,000	=	$1,600	+	$15,000
			$16,600				$16,600		

The asset Supplies is increased $1,600, and the liability
Accounts Payable is increased by the same amount.

TRANSACTION ANALYSIS
TRANSACTION 4

- Softbyte receives $1,200 cash from customers for programming services it has provided.
- This transaction represents the principal revenue-producing activity of Softbyte.

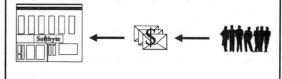

TRANSACTION ANALYSIS
TRANSACTION 4 SOLUTION

	Assets			=	Liabilities	+	Owner's Equity	
	Cash	+ Supplies	+ Equipment	=	Accounts Payable	+	R. Neal, Capital	
Old Bal.	$8,000	$1,600	$7,000		$1,600		$15,000	
(4)	+1,200						+1,200	Service Revenue
New Bal.	$9,200	+ $1,600	+ $7,000	=	$1,600	+	$16,200	
		$17,800				$17,800		

Cash is increased $1,200, and R. Neal, Capital is increased $1,200.

TRANSACTION ANALYSIS
TRANSACTION 5

Softbyte receives a bill for $250 from the Daily News for advertising the opening of its business but postpones payment of the bill until a later date.

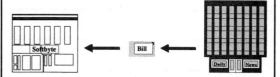

TRANSACTION ANALYSIS
TRANSACTION 5 SOLUTION

		Assets		=	Liabilities	+	Owner's Equity
	Cash	+ Supplies	+ Equipment	=	Accounts Payable	+	R. Neal, Capital
Old Bal.	$9,200	$1,600	$7,000	=	$1,600	+	$16,200
(5)					+250		-250 Advertising Expense
New Bal.	$9,200 +	$1,600 +	$7,000	=	$1,850	+	$15,950
		$17,800				$17,800	

Accounts Payable is increased $250, and R. Neal, Capital is decreased $250.

TRANSACTION ANALYSIS
TRANSACTION 6

- Softbyte provides programming services of $3,500 for customers.
- Cash amounting to $1,500 is received from customers, and the balance of $2,000 is billed to customers on account.

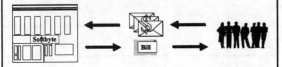

Softbyte   Bill

TRANSACTION ANALYSIS
TRANSACTION 6 SOLUTION

			Assets			=	Liabilities	+	Owner's Equity
	Cash	+ Accounts Receivable	+ Supplies	+ Equipment		=	Accounts Payable	+	R. Neal, Capital
Old Bal.	$ 9,200		$1,600	$7,000		=	$1,850		$15,950
(6)	+1,500	+2,000							+3,500 Service
New Bal.	$10,700 +	$2,000 +	$1,600 +	$7,000		=	$1,850	+	$19,450 Revenue
			$21,300					$21,300	

Cash is increased $1,500; Accounts Receivable is increased $2,000; and R. Neal, Capital is increased $3,500.

TRANSACTION ANALYSIS
TRANSACTION 7

Expenses paid in cash for September are store rent, $600, salaries of employees, $900, and utilities, $200.

Softbyte → $600
→ $900
→ $200

TRANSACTION ANALYSIS
TRANSACTION 7 SOLUTION

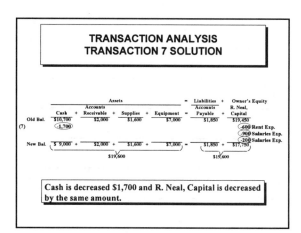

		Assets			=	Liabilities	+	Owner's Equity
	Cash	Accounts Receivable	Supplies	Equipment	=	Accounts Payable		R. Neal, Capital
Old Bal.	$10,700	$2,000	$1,600	$7,000	=	$1,850		$19,450
(7)	-1,700							-600 Rent Exp.
								-900 Salaries Exp.
								-200 Salaries Exp.
New Bal.	$ 9,000 +	$2,000 +	$1,600 +	$7,000	=	$1,850 +		$17,750
			$19,600				$19,600	

Cash is decreased $1,700 and R. Neal, Capital is decreased by the same amount.

TRANSACTION ANALYSIS
TRANSACTION 8

Softbyte pays its Daily News advertising bill of $250 in cash.

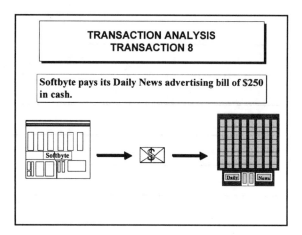

TRANSACTION ANALYSIS
TRANSACTION 8 SOLUTION

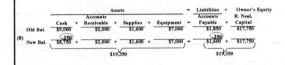

		Assets			=	Liabilities	+	Owner's Equity
		Accounts				Accounts		R. Neal,
	Cash +	Receivable +	Supplies +	Equipment	=	Payable	+	Capital
Old Bal.	$9,000	$2,000	$1,600	$7,000		$1,850		$17,750
(8)	–250					–250		
New Bal.	$8,750 +	$2,000 +	$1,600 +	$7,000	=	$1,600	+	$17,750
			$19,350				$19,350	

Cash is decreased $250 and Accounts Payable is decreased by the same amount.

TRANSACTION ANALYSIS
TRANSACTION 9

The sum of $600 in cash is received from customers who have previously been billed for services in Transaction 6.

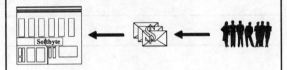

TRANSACTION ANALYSIS
TRANSACTION 9 SOLUTION

		Assets			=	Liabilities	+	Owner's Equity
		Accounts				Accounts		R. Neal,
	Cash +	Receivable +	Supplies +	Equipment	=	Payable	+	Capital
Old Bal.	$8,750	$2,000	$1,600	$7,000		$1,600		$17,750
(9)	+600	–600						
New Bal.	$9,350 +	$1,400 +	$1,600 +	$7,000	=	$1,600	+	$17,750
			$19,350				$19,350	

Cash is increased $600 and Accounts Receivable is decreased by the same amount.

TRANSACTION ANALYSIS
TRANSACTION 10

Ray Neal withdraws $1,300 in cash from the business for his personal use. action 6.

Softbyte → $1,300 →

TRANSACTION ANALYSIS
TRANSACTION 10 SOLUTION

	Assets				=	Liabilities	+	Owner's Equity
	Cash	+ Accounts Receivable	+ Supplies	+ Equipment	=	Accounts Payable	+	R. Neal, Capital
Old Bal.	$9,350	$1,400	$1,600	$7,000		$1,600		$17,750
(10)	-1,300							-1,300 Drawings
New Bal.	$8,050 +	$1,400 +	$1,600 +	$7,000	=	$1,600 +		$16,450
		$18,050				$18,050		

Cash is decreased $1,300 and R. Neal, Capital is decreased by the same amount.

STUDY OBJECTIVE 8

Prepare an income statement, owner's equity statement, balance sheet, and statement of cash flows.

FINANCIAL STATEMENTS

After transactions are identified, recorded, and summarized, 4 financial statements are prepared from the summarized accounting data:

1 An income statement presents the revenues and expenses and resulting net income or net loss of a company for a specific period of time.

2 An owner's equity statement summarizes the changes in owner's equity for a specific period of time.

3 A balance sheet reports the assets, liabilities, and owner's equity of a business enterprise at a specific date.

4 A statement of cash flows summarizes information concerning the cash inflows (receipts) and outflows (payments) for a specific period of time.

ILLUSTRATION 1-11
FINANCIAL STATEMENTS AND THEIR INTERRELATIONSHIPS

SOFTBYTE, INC.
Income Statement
For the Month Ended September 30, 1999

Revenues		
Service revenue		$ 4,700
Expenses		
Salaries expense	$ 900	
Rent expense	600	
Advertising expense	250	
Utilities expense	200	
Total expenses		1,950
Net income		2,750

Net income of $2,750 shown on the income statement is added to the beginning balance of owner's capital in the owner's equity statement.

ILLUSTRATION 1-11
FINANCIAL STATEMENTS AND THEIR INTERRELATIONSHIPS

SOFTBYTE, INC.
Owner's Equity Statement
For the Month Ended September 30, 1999

Retained earnings, September 1		$ –0–
Add: Investments	$ 15,000	
Net income	2,750	17,750
		17,750
Less: Drawings		1,300
Retained earnings, September 30		$ 16,450

Net income of $2,750 is determined from the information in the owner's equity column of the Summary of Transactions (Illustration 1-8).

ILLUSTRATION 1-11
FINANCIAL STATEMENTS AND THEIR INTERRELATIONSHIPS

SOFTBYTE, INC.
Owner's Equity Statement
For the Month Ended September 30, 1999

Retained earnings, September 1		$ –0–
Add: Investments	$ 15,000	
Net income	2,750	17,750
		17,750
Less: Drawings		1,300
Retained earnings, September 30		$16,450

Net income of $2,750 carried forward from the income statement to the owner's equity statement. The owner's capital of $16,450 at the end of the reporting period is shown as the final total of the owner's equity column of the Summary of Transactions (Illustration 1-8).

ILLUSTRATION 1-11
FINANCIAL STATEMENTS AND THEIR INTERRELATIONSHIPS

SOFTBYTE, INC.
Balance Sheet
September 30, 1999
Assets

Cash	$ 8,050
Accounts receivable	1,400
Supplies	1,600
Equipment	7,000
Total assets	$ 18,050

Liabilities and Owner's Equity

Liabilities	
Accounts payable	$ 1,600
Owner's equity	
R. Neal, capital	16,450
Total liabilities and owner's equity	$ 18,050

Owner's capital of $16,450 at the end of the reporting period shown in the owner's equity statement is shown on the balance sheet.

ILLUSTRATION 1-11
FINANCIAL STATEMENTS AND THEIR INTERRELATIONSHIPS

SOFTBYTE, INC.
Balance Sheet
September 30, 1999
Assets

Cash	$ 8,050
Accounts receivable	1,400
Supplies	1,600
Equipment	7,000
Total assets	$ 18,050

Liabilities and Owner's Equity

Liabilities	
Accounts payable	$ 1,600
Owner's equity	
R. Neal, capital	16,450
Total liabilities and owner's equity	$ 18,050

Cash of $8,050 on the balance sheet is reported on the statement of cash flows.

ILLUSTRATION 1-11
FINANCIAL STATEMENTS AND THEIR INTERRELATIONSHIPS

SOFTBYTE, INC.
Statement of Cash Flows
For the Month Ended September 30, 1999

Cash flows from operating activities		
Cash receipts from revenues		$ 3,300
Cash payments for expenses		(1,950)
Net cash provided by operating activities		1,350
Cash flows from investing activities		
Purchase of equipment		(7,000)
Cash flows from financing activities		
Sale of common stock	$ 15,000	
Payment of cash dividends	(1,300)	
Net cash provided by financing activities		13,700
Net increase in cash		8,050
Cash at the beginning of the period		–0–
Cash at the end of the period		$ 8,050

Cash of $8,050 on the balance sheet and statement of cash flows is shown as the final total of the cash column of the Summary of Transactions (Illustration 1-8).

CHAPTER 1
ACCOUNTING IN ACTION

WILEY
Publishers Since 1807

Accounting Principles, 5e
Weygandt, Kieso, & Kimmel

Prepared by
Marianne Bradford
The University of Tennessee
Gregory K. Lowry
Macon Technical Institute

John Wiley & Sons, Inc.

CHAPTER 2
THE RECORDING PROCESS

After studying this chapter, you should be able to:

1 Explain what an account is and how it helps in the recording process.

2 Define debits and credits and explain how they are used to record business transactions.

3 Identify the basic steps in the recording process.

4 Explain what a journal is and how it helps in the recording process.

CHAPTER 2
THE RECORDING PROCESS

After studying this chapter, you should be able to:

5 Explain what a ledger is and how it helps in the recording process.

6 Explain what posting is and how it helps in the recording process.

7 Prepare a trial balance and explain its purpose.

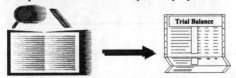

Trial Balance

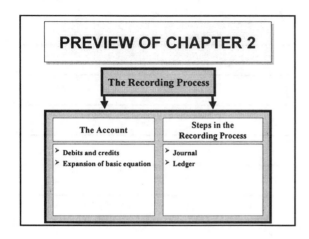

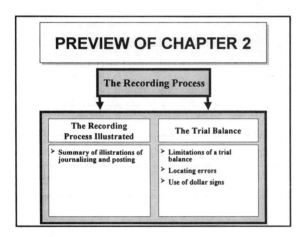

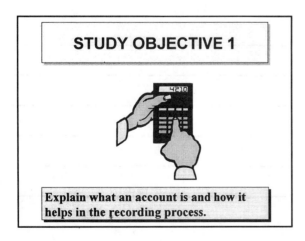

Chapter 2: The Recording Process

- An account is an individual accounting record of increases and decreases in a specific asset, liability, or owner's equity item.
- A company will have separate accounts for such items as cash, salaries expense, accounts payable, and so on.

STUDY OBJECTIVE 2

Define debits and credits and explain how they are used to record business transactions.

ILLUSTRATION 2-1
BASIC FORM OF ACCOUNT

- In its simplest form, an account consists of
  1 the title of the account,
  2 a left or debit side, and
  3 a right or credit side.
- The alignment of these parts resembles the letter T, and therefore the account form is called a T account.

Title of Account	
Left or debit side	Right or credit side
Debit balance	Credit balance

DEBITS AND CREDITS

- The terms debit and credit mean left and right, respectively.
- The act of entering an amount on the left side of an account is called debiting the account and making an entry on the right side is crediting the account.
- When the debit amounts exceed the credits, an account has a debit balance; when the reverse is true, the account has a credit balance.

ILLUSTRATION 2-2
TABULAR SUMMARY COMPARED TO ACCOUNT FORM

Tabular Summary

Cash
$15,000
- 7,000
1,200
1,500
- 1,700
- 250
600
- 1,300
$ 8,050

Account Form

Cash	
Debit	Credit
15,000	7,000
1,200	1,700
1,500	250
600	1,300
Balance 8,050	

DEBITING AN ACCOUNT

Cash	
Debits	Credits
15,000	

Example: The owner makes an initial investment of $15,000 to start the business. Cash is debited as the owner's Capital is credited.

CREDITING AN ACCOUNT

Cash	
Debits	Credits
	7,000

Example: Monthly rent of $7,000 is paid. Cash is credited as Rent Expense is debited.

DEBITING AND CREDITING AN ACCOUNT

Cash	
Debits	Credits
15,000	7,000
8,000	

Example: Cash is debited for $15,000 and credited for $7,000, leaving a debit balance of $8,000.

DOUBLE-ENTRY SYSTEM

- In a double-entry system, equal debits and credits are made in the accounts for each transaction.
- Thus, the total debits will always equal the total credits and the accounting equation will always stay in balance.

Assets ✚ Liabilities ⚌ Equity

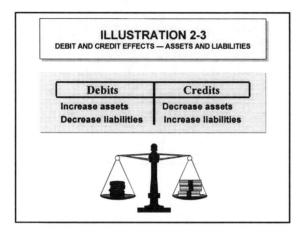

NORMAL BALANCE

- Every account classification has a normal balance, whether it is a debit or credit.
- For that particular account, the opposite side entries should never exceed the normal balance.

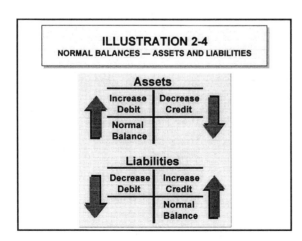

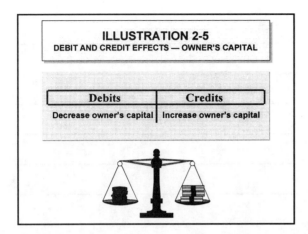

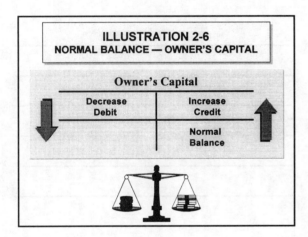

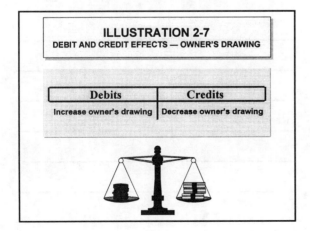

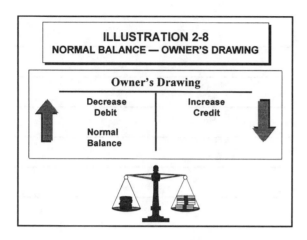

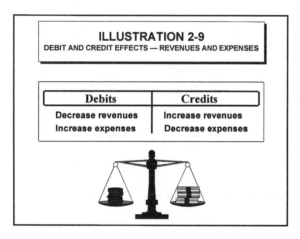

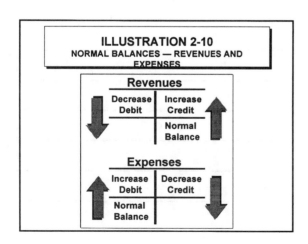

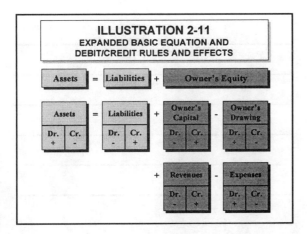

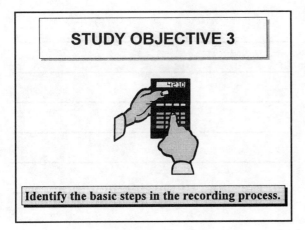

STEPS IN THE RECORDING PROCESS

The basic steps in the recording process are:

1 Analyze each transaction in terms of its effect on the accounts.

2 Enter the transaction information in a journal (book of original entry).

3 Transfer the journal information to the appropriate accounts in the ledger (book of accounts).

ILLUSTRATION 2-12
THE RECORDING PROCESS

1 Analyze each transaction

2 Enter transaction in a journal

3 Transfer journal information to ledger accounts

STUDY OBJECTIVE 4

Explain what a journal is and how it helps in the recording process.

THE JOURNAL

- Transactions are initially recorded in chronological order in a journal before being transferred to the accounts.
- Every company has a general journal which contains:
  1 spaces for dates,
  2 account titles and explanations,
  3 references, and
  4 two money columns.

THE JOURNAL

The journal makes several significant contributions to the recording process:

1 It discloses in one place the complete effect of a transaction.

2 It provides a chronological record of transactions.

3 It helps to prevent or locate errors because the debit and credit amounts for each entry can be readily compared.

JOURNALIZING

- Entering transaction data in the journal is known as journalizing.
- Separate journal entries are made for each transaction.
- A complete entry consists of:

  1 the date of the transaction,

  2 the accounts and amounts to be debited and credited, and

  3 a brief explanation of the transaction.

ILLUSTRATION 2-13
TECHNIQUE OF JOURNALIZING

The date of the transaction is entered in the date column.

GENERAL JOURNAL				J1
Date	Account Titles and Explanation	Ref.	Debit	Credit
1999 Sept. 1	Cash		15,000	
	R. Neal, Capital			15,000
	(Invested cash in business)			
1	Computer Equipment		7,000	
	Cash			7,000
	(Purchased equipment for cash)			

ILLUSTRATION 2-13
TECHNIQUE OF JOURNALIZING

The debit account title is entered at the extreme left margin of the Account Titles and Explanation column. The credit account title is indented on the next line.

GENERAL JOURNAL   J1

Date	Account Titles and Explanation	Ref.	Debit	Credit
1999				
Sept. 1	Cash		15,000	
	R. Neal, Capital			15,000
	(Invested cash in business)			
1	Computer Equipment		7,000	
	Cash			7,000
	(Purchased equipment for cash)			

ILLUSTRATION 2-13
TECHNIQUE OF JOURNALIZING

The amounts for the debits are recorded in the Debit column and the amounts for the credits are recorded in the Credit column.

GENERAL JOURNAL   J1

Date	Account Titles and Explanation	Ref.	Debit	Credit
1999				
Sept. 1	Cash		15,000	
	R. Neal, Capital			15,000
	(Invested cash in business)			
1	Computer Equipment		7,000	
	Cash			7,000
	(Purchased equipment for cash)			

ILLUSTRATION 2-13
TECHNIQUE OF JOURNALIZING

A brief explanation of the transaction is given.

GENERAL JOURNAL   J1

Date	Account Titles and Explanation	Ref.	Debit	Credit
1999				
Sept. 1	Cash		15,000	
	R. Neal, Capital			15,000
	(Invested cash in business)			
1	Computer Equipment		7,000	
	Cash			7,000
	(Purchased equipment for cash)			

ILLUSTRATION 2-13
TECHNIQUE OF JOURNALIZING

A space is left between journal entries. The blank space separates individual journal entries and makes the entire journal easier to read.

GENERAL JOURNAL				J1
Date	Account Titles and Explanation	Ref.	Debit	Credit
1999 Sept. 1	Cash		15,000	
	R. Neal, Capital			15,000
	(Invested cash in business)			
1	Computer Equipment		7,000	
	Cash			7,000
	(Purchased equipment for cash)			

ILLUSTRATION 2-13
TECHNIQUE OF JOURNALIZING

The column entitled Ref. is left blank at the time journal entry is made and is used later when the journal entries are transferred to the ledger accounts.

GENERAL JOURNAL				J1
Date	Account Titles and Explanation	Ref.	Debit	Credit
1999 Sept. 1	Cash		15,000	
	R. Neal, Capital			15,000
	(Invested cash in business)			
1	Computer Equipment		7,000	
	Cash			7,000
	(Purchased equipment for cash)			

SIMPLE AND COMPOUND JOURNAL ENTRIES

If an entry involves only two accounts, one debit and one credit, it is considered a simple entry.

GENERAL JOURNAL				J1
Date	Account Titles and Explanation	Ref.	Debit	Credit
1999 July 1	Cash		20,000	
	K. Browne, Capital			20,000
	(Invested cash in the business)			

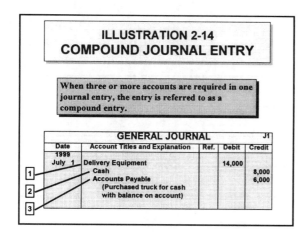

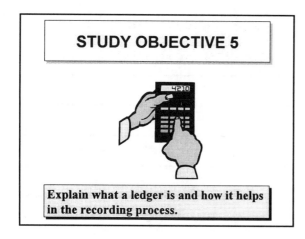

STUDY OBJECTIVE 5

Explain what a ledger is and how it helps in the recording process.

THE LEDGER

- The entire group of accounts maintained by a company is referred to collectively as the ledger.
- A general ledger contains all the assets, liabilities, and owner's equity accounts.

ILLUSTRATION 2-15
THE GENERAL LEDGER

Individual Assets	Individual Liabilities	Individual Owner's Equity

Equipment	Interest Payable	Salaries Payable
Land	Salaries Payable	Fees Earned
Supplies	Accounts Payable	J. Lind, Drawing
Cash	Notes Payable	J. Lind, Capital

STUDY OBJECTIVE 6

Explain what posting is and how it helps in the recording process.

ILLUSTRATION 2-17
POSTING A JOURNAL ENTRY

GENERAL JOURNAL   J1

Date	Account Titles and Explanation	Ref.	Debit	Credit
1999 Sept. 1	Cash	10	15,000	
	R. Neal, Capital	25		15,000
	(invested cash in business)			

GENERAL LEDGER

CASH   NO. 10

Date	Explanation	Ref.	Debit	Credit	Balance
1999 Sept. 1		J1	15,000		15,000

R. NEAL, CAPITAL   NO. 25

Date	Explanation	Ref.	Debit	Credit	Balance
1999 Sept. 1		J1		15,000	15,000

In the ledger, enter in the appropriate columns of the account(s)
debited the date, journal page, and debit amount shown in the journal.

ILLUSTRATION 2-17
POSTING A JOURNAL ENTRY

GENERAL JOURNAL   J1

Date	Account Titles and Explanation	Ref.	Debit	Credit
1999 Sept. 1	Cash	10	15,000	
	R. Neal, Capital	25		15,000
	(invested cash in business)			

GENERAL LEDGER

CASH   NO. 10

Date	Explanation	Ref.	Debit	Credit	Balance
1999 Sept. 1		J1	15,000		15,000

R. NEAL, CAPITAL   NO. 25

Date	Explanation	Ref.	Debit	Credit	Balance
1999 Sept. 1		J1		15,000	15,000

In the reference column of the journal, write the account
number to which the debit amount was posted.

ILLUSTRATION 2-17
POSTING A JOURNAL ENTRY

GENERAL JOURNAL   J1

Date	Account Titles and Explanation	Ref.	Debit	Credit
1999 Sept. 1	Cash	10	15,000	
	R. Neal, Capital	25		15,000
	(invested cash in business)			

GENERAL LEDGER

CASH   NO. 10

Date	Explanation	Ref.	Debit	Credit	Balance
1999 Sept. 1		J1	15,000		15,000

R. NEAL, CAPITAL   NO. 25

Date	Explanation	Ref.	Debit	Credit	Balance
1999 Sept. 1		J1		15,000	15,000

In the ledger, enter in the appropriate columns of the account(s) credited
the date, journal page, and credit amount shown in the journal.

ILLUSTRATION 2-17
POSTING A JOURNAL ENTRY

GENERAL JOURNAL   J1

Date	Account Titles and Explanation	Ref.	Debit	Credit
1999 Sept. 1	Cash	(10)	15,000	
	R. Neal, Capital			15,000
	(Invested cash in business)			

GENERAL LEDGER

CASH   NO. 10

Date	Explanation	Ref.	Debit	Credit	Balance
1999 Sept. 1		J1	15,000		15,000

R. NEAL, CAPITAL   NO. 25

Date	Explanation	Ref.	Debit	Credit	Balance
1999 Sept. 1		J1		15,000	15,000

In the reference column of the journal, write the account number to which the credit amount was posted.

ILLUSTRATION 2-18
CHART OF ACCOUNTS

Most companies have a chart of accounts that lists the accounts and the account numbers which identify their location in the ledger.

Pioneer Advertising Agency

Assets
1. Cash
6. Accounts Receivable
8. Advertising Supplies
10. Prepaid Insurance
15. Office Equipment
16. Accumulated Depreciation — Office Equipment

Liabilities
25. Notes Payable
26. Accounts Payable
27. Interest Payable
28. Unearned Fees
29. Salaries Payable

Owner's Equity
40. C.R. Byrd, Capital
41. C.R. Byrd, Drawing
49. Income Summary

Revenues
50. Fees Earned

Expenses
60. Salaries Expense
61. Advertising Supplies Expense
62. Rent Expense
63. Insurance Expense
64. Interest Expense
65. Depreciation Expense

ILLUSTRATION 2-19
INVESTMENT OF CASH BY OWNER

Transaction	October 1, C.R. Byrd invests $10,000 cash in an advertising venture to be known as the Pioneer Advertising Agency.
Basic Analysis	The asset Cash is increased $10,000, and owner's equity C. R. Byrd, Capital is increased $10,000.
Debit-Credit Analysis	Debits increase assets: debit Cash $10,000. Credits increase owner's equity: credit C.R. Byrd, Capital $10,000.

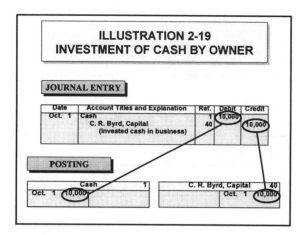

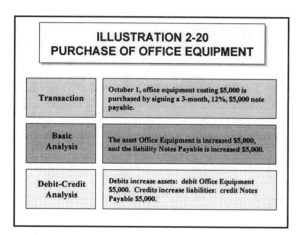

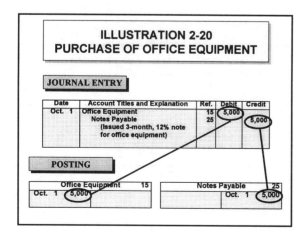

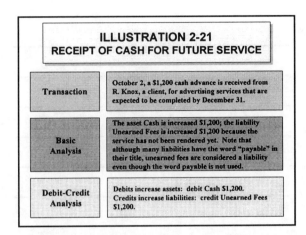

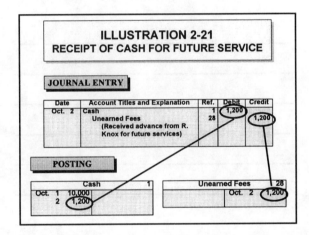

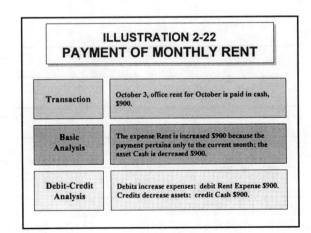

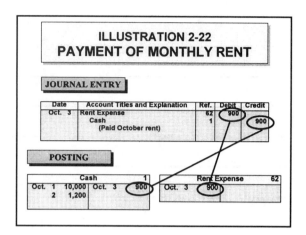

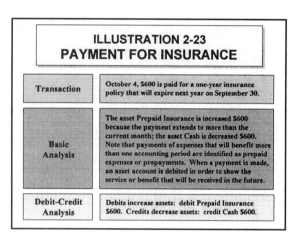

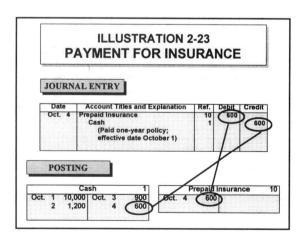

ILLUSTRATION 2-24
PURCHASE OF SUPPLIES ON CREDIT

Transaction	October 5, an estimated 3-month supply of advertising materials is purchased on account from Aero Supply for $2,500.
Basic Analysis	The asset Advertising Supplies is increased $2,500; the liability Accounts Payable is increased $2,500.
Debit-Credit Analysis	Debits increase assets: debit Advertising Supplies $2,500. Credits increase liabilities: credit Accounts Payable $2,500.

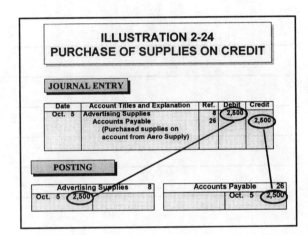

ILLUSTRATION 2-24
PURCHASE OF SUPPLIES ON CREDIT

JOURNAL ENTRY

Date	Account Titles and Explanation	Ref.	Debit	Credit
Oct. 5	Advertising Supplies	8	2,500	
	Accounts Payable	26		2,500
	(Purchased supplies on account from Aero Supply)			

POSTING

Advertising Supplies	8
Oct. 5 2,500	

Accounts Payable	26
	Oct. 5 2,500

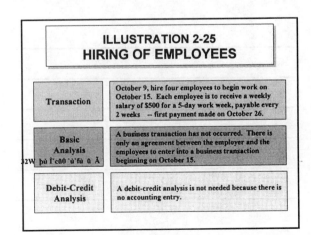

ILLUSTRATION 2-25
HIRING OF EMPLOYEES

Transaction	October 9, hire four employees to begin work on October 15. Each employee is to receive a weekly salary of $500 for a 5-day work week, payable every 2 weeks -- first payment made on October 26.
Basic Analysis	A business transaction has not occurred. There is only an agreement between the employer and the employees to enter into a business transaction beginning on October 15.
Debit-Credit Analysis	A debit-credit analysis is not needed because there is no accounting entry.

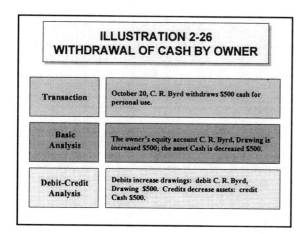

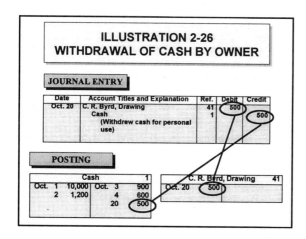

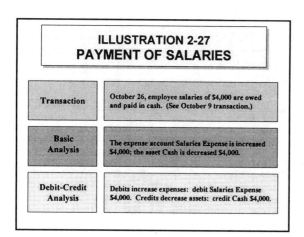

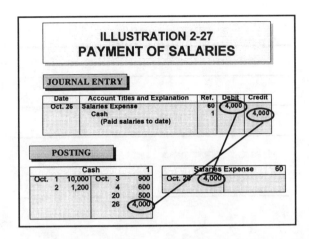

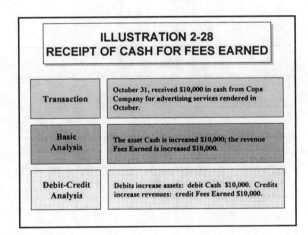

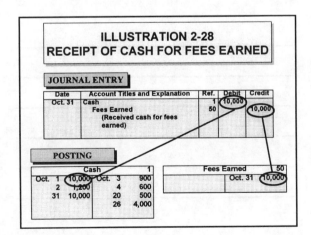

STUDY OBJECTIVE 7

Prepare a trial balance and explain its purposes.

THE TRIAL BALANCE

- A trial balance is a list of accounts and their balances at a given time.
- The primary purpose of a trial balance is to prove the mathematical equality of debits and credits after posting.
- A trial balance also uncovers errors in journalizing and posting.
- The procedures for preparing a trial balance consist of:
  1 Listing the account titles and their balances.
  2 Totaling the debit and credit columns.
  3 Proving the equality of the two columns.

ILLUSTRATION 2-31
A TRIAL BALANCE

PIONEER ADVERTISING AGENCY
Trial Balance
October 31, 1999

	Debit	Credit
Cash	$ 15,200	
Advertising Supplies	2,500	
Prepaid Insurance	600	
Office Equipment	5,000	
Notes Payable		$ 5,000
Accounts Payable		2,500
Unearned Fees		1,200
C. R. Byrd, Capital		10,000
C. R. Byrd, Drawing	500	
Fees Earned		10,000
Salaries Expense	4,000	
Rent Expense	900	
	$ 28,700	$ 28,700

The total debits must equal the total credits.

LIMITATIONS OF A TRIAL BALANCE

- A trial balance does not prove that all transactions have been recorded or that the ledger is correct.
- Numerous errors may exist even though the trial balance columns agree.
- The trial balance may balance even when:
    1 a transaction is not journalized,
    2 a correct journal entry is not posted,
    3 a journal entry is posted twice,
    4 incorrect accounts are used in journalizing or posting, or
    5 offsetting errors are made in recording the amount of the transaction.

CHAPTER 2
THE RECORDING PROCESS

WILEY

Publishers Since 1807

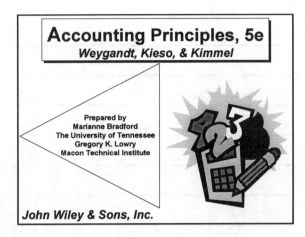

Accounting Principles, 5e
Weygandt, Kieso, & Kimmel

Prepared by
Marianne Bradford
The University of Tennessee
Gregory K. Lowry
Macon Technical Institute

John Wiley & Sons, Inc.

CHAPTER 3
ADJUSTING THE ACCOUNTS

After studying this chapter, you should be able to:

1 Explain the time period assumption.
2 Distinguish between the revenue recognition principle and the matching principle.
3 Explain why adjusting entries are needed.
4 Identify the major types of adjusting entries.
5 Prepare adjusting entries for prepayments.
6 Prepare adjusting entries for accruals.
7 Describe the nature and purpose of an adjusted trial balance.
8 Explain the accrual basis of accounting.
9 Prepare adjusting entries for the alternative treatment of prepayments.

PREVIEW OF CHAPTER 3

Adjusting the Acccounts

Timing Issues	The Basics of Adjusting Entries
➤ Time period assumption	➤ Types of adjusting entries
➤ Fiscal and calendar years	➤ Adjusting entries for prepayments
➤ Recoognizing revenues and expenses	➤ Adjusting entries for accruals
	➤ Summary

PREVIEW OF CHAPTER 3

Adjusting the
Acccounts

The Adjusted Trial Balance and Financial Statements	Accrual vs. Cash Basis of Accounting
➢ Preparing the adjusted trial balance ➢ Preparing financial statements	

STUDY OBJECTIVE 1

Explain the time period assumption.

TIME-PERIOD ASSUMPTION

- The time period (or periodicity) assumption assumes that the economic life of a business can be divided into artificial time periods.
- Accounting time periods are generally a month, a quarter, or a year.
- The accounting time period of one year in length is usually known as a fiscal year.

STUDY OBJECTIVE 2

Distinguish between the revenue recognition principle and the matching principle.

REVENUE RECOGNITION PRINCIPLE

- The revenue recognition principle states that revenue should be recognized in the accounting period in which it is earned.
- In a service business, revenue is considered to be earned at the time the service is performed.

THE MATCHING PRINCIPLE

- The practice of expense recognition is referred to as the matching principle.
- The matching principle dictates that efforts (expenses) be matched with accomplishments (revenues).

Revenues earned this month

are offset against....

expenses incurred in earning the revenue

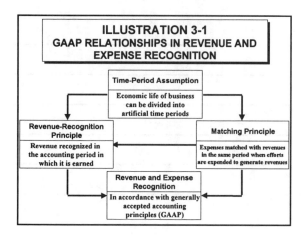

ILLUSTRATION 3-1
GAAP RELATIONSHIPS IN REVENUE AND
EXPENSE RECOGNITION

STUDY OBJECTIVE 3

Explain why adjusting entries are needed.

ADJUSTING ENTRIES

Adjusting entries are made in order for:

1 Revenues to be recorded in the period in which they are *earned*, and for......

2 Expenses to be recognized in the period in which they are *incurred*.

STUDY OBJECTIVE 4

Identify the major types of adjusting entries.

ADJUSTING ENTRIES

- Adjusting entries are required each time financial statements are prepared.
- Adjusting entries can be classified as
  1 prepayments (*prepaid expenses* or *unearned revenues*) OR
  2 accruals (*accrued revenues* or *accrued expenses*)

TYPES OF ADJUSTING ENTRIES

Prepayments

1 Prepaid Expenses — Expenses paid in cash and recorded as assets before they are used or consumed

2 Unearned Revenues — Revenues received in cash and recorded as liabilities before they are earned

TYPES OF ADJUSTING ENTRIES

Accruals

1 Accrued Revenues — Revenues earned but not yet received in cash or recorded

2 Accrued Expenses — Expenses incurred but not yet paid in cash or recorded

---

ILLUSTRATION 3-3
TRIAL BALANCE

PIONEER ADVERTISING AGENCY
Trial Balance
October 31, 1999

	Debit	Credit
Cash	$ 15,200	
Advertising Supplies	2,500	
Prepaid Insurance	600	
Office Equipment	5,000	
Notes Payable		$ 5,000
Accounts Payable		2,500
Unearned Revenue		1,200
C. R. Byrd, Capital		10,000
C. R. Byrd, Drawing	500	
Service Revenue		10,000
Salaries Expense	4,000	
Rent Expense	900	
	$ 28,700	$ 28,700

The Trial Balance is the starting place for adjusting entries.

STUDY OBJECTIVE 5

Prepare adjusting entries for prepayments.

PREPAYMENTS

- Prepayments are either prepaid expenses or unearned revenues.
- Adjusting entries for prepayments are required to record the portion of the prepayment that represents

  1 the expense incurred or

  2 the revenue earned in the current accounting period.

ILLUSTRATION 3-4
ADJUSTING ENTRIES FOR PREPAYMENTS

Adjusting Entries

Prepaid Expenses

Asset		Expense	
Unadjusted Balance	Credit Adjusting Entry (-)	Debit Adjusting Entry (+)	

Unearned Revenues

Liability		Revenue	
Debit Adjusting Entry (-)	Unadjusted Balance		Credit Adjusting Entry (+)

PREPAID EXPENSES

- Prepaid expenses are expenses paid in cash and recorded as assets before they are used or consumed.
- Prepaid expenses expire with the passage of time or through use and consumption.
- An *asset-expense account relationship* exists with prepaid expenses.

PREPAID EXPENSES

- Prior to adjustment, assets are overstated and expenses are understated.
- The adjusting entry results in a debit to an expense account and a credit to an asset account.
- Examples of prepaid expenses include supplies, insurance, and depreciation.

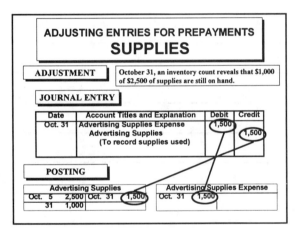

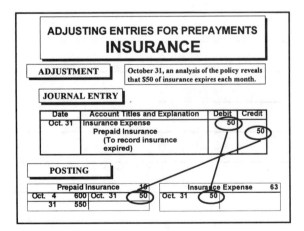

DEPRECIATION

- Depreciation is the process of allocating the cost of an asset to expense over its useful life in a rational and systematic manner.
- The purchase of equipment or a building is viewed as a long-term prepayment of services and, therefore, is allocated in the same manner as other prepaid expenses.

DEPRECIATION

- Depreciation is an estimate rather than a factual measurement of the cost that has expired.
- In recording depreciation, *Depreciation Expense* is debited and a contra asset account, *Accumulated Depreciation*, is credited

Depreciation Expense		Accumulated Depreciation	
xxx			xxx

DEPRECIATION

- In the balance sheet, Accumulated Depreciation is offset against the asset account.
- The difference between the cost of the asset and its related accumulated depreciation is referred to as the book value of the asset.

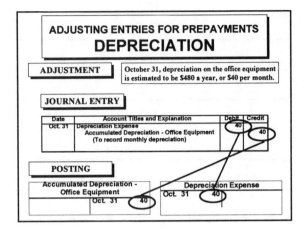

UNEARNED REVENUES

- Unearned revenues are revenues received and recorded as liabilities before they are earned.
- Unearned revenues are subsequently earned by rendering a service to a customer.
- A *liability-revenue* account relationship exists with unearned revenues.

UNEARNED REVENUES

- Prior to adjustment, liabilities are overstated and revenues are understated.
- The adjusting entry results in a debit to a liability account and a credit to a revenue account.
- Examples of unearned revenues include rent, magazine subscriptions, and customer deposits for future services.

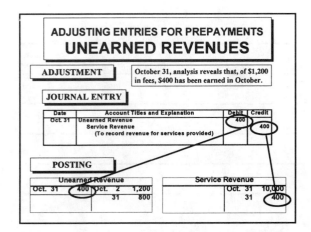

ADJUSTING ENTRIES FOR PREPAYMENTS
UNEARNED REVENUES

ADJUSTMENT | October 31, analysis reveals that, of $1,200 in fees, $400 has been earned in October.

JOURNAL ENTRY

Date	Account Titles and Explanation	Debit	Credit
Oct. 31	Unearned Revenue	400	
	Service Revenue		400
	(To record revenue for services provided)		

POSTING

Unearned Revenue			Service Revenue	
Oct. 31 400	Oct. 2 1,200			Oct. 31 10,000
	31 800			31 400

STUDY OBJECTIVE 6

Prepare adjusting entries for accruals.

ACCRUALS

- The second category of adjusting entries is accruals.
- Adjusting entries for accruals are required to record revenues earned and expenses incurred in the current period.
- The adjusting entry for accruals will increase both a balance sheet and an income statement account.

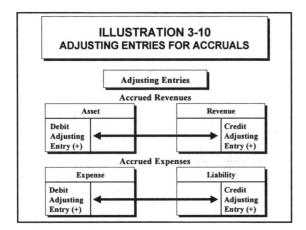

ILLUSTRATION 3-10
ADJUSTING ENTRIES FOR ACCRUALS

Adjusting Entries

Accrued Revenues

Asset			Revenue
Debit Adjusting Entry (+)			Credit Adjusting Entry (+)

Accrued Expenses

Expense			Liability
Debit Adjusting Entry (+)			Credit Adjusting Entry (+)

ACCRUED REVENUES

- Accrued revenues may accumulate with the passing of time or through services performed but not billed or collected.
- An asset-revenue account relationship exists with accrued revenues.
- Prior to adjustment, assets and revenues are understated.
- The adjusting entry requires a debit to an asset account and a credit to a revenue account.

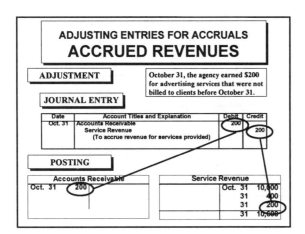

ADJUSTING ENTRIES FOR ACCRUALS
ACCRUED REVENUES

ADJUSTMENT   October 31, the agency earned $200 for advertising services that were not billed to clients before October 31.

JOURNAL ENTRY

Date	Account Titles and Explanation	Debit	Credit
Oct. 31	Accounts Receivable	200	
	Service Revenue		200
	(To accrue revenue for services provided)		

POSTING

Accounts Receivable		Service Revenue	
Oct. 31 200		Oct. 31	10,600
		31	400
		31	200
		31	10,600

ACCRUED EXPENSES

- Accrued expenses are expenses incurred but not paid yet.
- A liability-expense account relationship exists
- Prior to adjustment, liabilities and expenses are understated
- The Adjusting Entry results in a debit to an expense account and a credit to a liability account

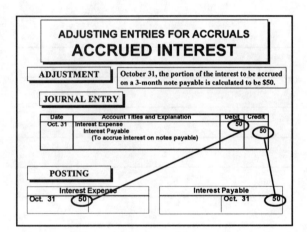

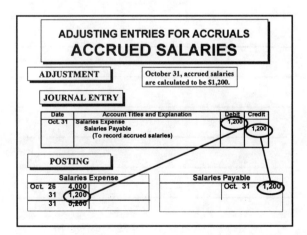

ILLUSTRATION 3-15
SUMMARY OF ADJUSTING ENTRIES

Type of Adjustment	Account Relationship	Accounts before Adjustment	Adjusting Entry
1 Prepaid expenses	Assets and expenses	Assets overstated Expenses understated	Dr. Expenses Cr. Assets
2 Unearned revenues	Liabilities and revenues	Liabilities overstated Revenues understated	Dr. Liabilities Cr. Revenues
3 Accrued revenues	Assets and revenues	Assets understated Revenues understated	Dr. Assets Cr. Revenues
4 Accrued expenses	Expenses and liabilities	Expenses understated Liabilities understated	Dr. Expenses Cr. Liabilities

STUDY OBJECTIVE 7

Describe the nature and purpose of an adjusted trial balance.

ADJUSTED TRIAL BALANCE

- An Adjusted Trial Balance is prepared after all adjusting entries have been journalized and posted.
- It shows the balances of all accounts at the end of the accounting period and the effects of all financial events that have occurred during the period.
- It proves the equality of the total debit and credit balances in the ledger after all adjustments have been made.
- Financial statements can be prepared directly from the adjusted trial balance.

ILLUSTRATION 3-18
TRIAL BALANCE AND ADJUSTED TRIAL BALANCE COMPARED

PIONEER ADVERTISING AGENCY
Trial Balances
October 31, 1999

	Before Adjustment		After Adjustment	
	Debit	Credit	Debit	Credit
Cash	$ 15,200		$ 15,200	
Accounts Receivable			200	
Advertising Supplies	2,500		1,000	
Prepaid Insurance	600		550	
Office Equipment	5,000		5,000	
Accumulated Depreciation - Office Equipment				$ 40
Notes Payable		$ 5,000		5,000
Accounts Payable		2,500		2,500
Interest Payable				50
Unearned Revenue		1,200		800
Salaries Payable				1,200
C. R. Byrd, Capital		10,000		10,000
C. R. Byrd, Drawing	500		500	
Service Revenue		10,000		10,600
Salaries Expense	4,000		5,200	
Advertising Supplies Expense			1,500	
Rent Expense	900		900	
Insurance Expense			50	
Interest Expense			50	
Depreciation Expense			40	
	$ 28,700	$ 28,700	$ 30,190	$ 30,190

PREPARING FINANCIAL STATEMENTS

Financial statements can be prepared directly from an adjusted trial balance.

1 The income statement is prepared from the revenue and expense accounts.

2 The owner's equity statement is derived from the owner's capital and drawing accounts and the net income (or net loss) shown in the income statement.

3 The balance sheet is then prepared from the asset and liability accounts and the ending owner's capital balance as reported in the owner's equity statement.

ILLUSTRATION 3-19
PREPARATION OF THE INCOME STATEMENT AND THE OWNER'S EQUITY STATEMENT FROM THE ADJUSTED TRIAL BALANCE

PIONEER ADVERTISING AGENCY
Adjusted Trial Balance
October 31, 1999

	Debit	Credit
Cash	$ 15,200	
Accounts Receivable	200	
Advertising Supplies	1,000	
Prepaid Insurance	550	
Office Equipment	5,000	
Accumulated Depreciation - Office Equipment		$ 40
Notes Payable		5,000
Accounts Payable		2,500
Interest Payable		50
Unearned Revenue		800
Salaries Payable		1,200
C. R. Byrd, Capital		10,000
C. R. Byrd, Drawing	500	
Service Revenue		10,600
Salaries Expense	5,200	
Advertising Supplies Expense	1,500	
Rent Expense	900	
Insurance Expense	50	
Interest Expense	50	
Depreciation Expense	40	
	$ 30,190	$ 30,190

ILLUSTRATION 3-19
PREPARATION OF THE INCOME STATEMENT AND THE OWNER'S EQUITY STATEMENT FROM THE ADJUSTED TRIAL BALANCE

PIONEER ADVERTISING AGENCY
Income Statement
For the Month Ended October 31, 1999

Revenues		
Fees earned		$ 10,600
Expenses		
Salaries expense	$ 5,200	
Advertising supplies expense	1,500	
Rent expense	900	
Insurance expense	50	
Interest expense	50	
Depreciation expense	40	
Total expenses		7,740
Net income		$ 2,860

The income statement is prepared from the revenue and expense accounts.

ILLUSTRATION 3-19
PREPARATION OF THE INCOME STATEMENT AND THE OWNER'S EQUITY STATEMENT FROM THE ADJUSTED TRIAL BALANCE

PIONEER ADVERTISING AGENCY
Adjusted Trial Balance
October 31, 1999

	Debit	Credit
Cash	$ 15,200	
Accounts Receivable	200	
Advertising Supplies	1,000	
Prepaid Insurance	550	
Office Equipment	5,000	
Accumulated Depreciation - Office Equipment		$ 40
Notes Payable		5,000
Accounts Payable		2,500
Interest Payable		50
Unearned Revenue		800
Salaries Payable		1,200
C. R. Byrd, Capital		10,000
C. R. Byrd, Drawing	500	
Service Revenue		10,600
Salaries Expense	5,200	
Advertising Supplies Expense	1,500	
Rent Expense	900	
Insurance Expense	50	
Interest Expense	50	
Depreciation Expense	40	
	$ 30,190	$ 30,190

ILLUSTRATION 3-19
PREPARATION OF THE INCOME STATEMENT AND THE OWNER'S EQUITY STATEMENT FROM THE ADJUSTED TRIAL BALANCE

PIONEER ADVERTISING AGENCY
Owner's Equity Statement
For the Month Ended October 31, 1999

C.R. Byrd, Capital, October 1		$ -0-
Add: Investments	$ 10,000	
Net income	2,860	12,860
		12,860
Less: Drawings		500
C.R. Byrd, Capital, October 31		$ 12,360

The owner's equity statement is prepared from the owner's capital and drawing accounts and the net income (or net loss) shown in the income statement.

ILLUSTRATION 3-20
PREPARATION OF THE BALANCE SHEET FROM THE ADJUSTED TRIAL BALANCE

PIONEER ADVERTISING AGENCY
Adjusted Trial Balance
October 31, 1999

	Debit	Credit
Cash	$ 15,200	
Accounts Receivable	200	
Advertising Supplies	1,000	
Prepaid Insurance	550	
Office Equipment	5,000	
Accumulated Depreciation - Office Equipment		$ 40
Notes Payable		5,000
Accounts Payable		2,500
Interest Payable		50
Unearned Revenue		800
Salaries Payable		1,200
C. R. Byrd, Capital		10,000
C. R. Byrd, Drawing	500	
Service Revenue		10,600
Salaries Expense	5,200	
Advertising Supplies Expense	1,500	
Rent Expense	900	
Insurance Expense	50	
Interest Expense	50	
Depreciation Expense	40	
	$ 30,190	$ 30,190

ILLUSTRATION 3-20
PREPARATION OF THE BALANCE SHEET FROM THE ADJUSTED TRIAL BALANCE

PIONEER ADVERTISING AGENCY
Balance Sheet
October 31, 1996

Assets			Liabilities and Owner's Equity	
Cash		$ 15,200	Liabilities	
Accounts receivable		200	Notes payable	$ 5,000
Advertising supplies		1,000	Accounts payable	2,500
Prepaid insurance		550	Interest payable	50
Office equipment	$ 5,000		Unearned fees	800
Less: Accumulated			Salaries payable	1,200
depreciation	40	4,960	Total liabilities	9,550
			Owner's equity	
			C.R. Byrd, Capital	12,360
			Total liabilities and owner's	
Total assets		$ 21,910	equity	$ 21,910

The balance sheet is then prepared from the asset and liability accounts and the ending owner's capital balance as reported in the owner's equity statement.

STUDY OBJECTIVE 8

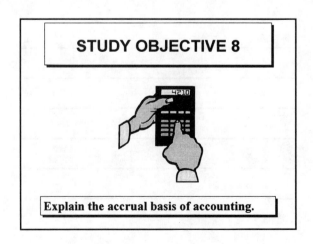

Explain the accrual basis of accounting.

ACCRUAL BASIS OF ACCOUNTING

- The revenue recognition and matching principles are used under the accrual basis of accounting.
- Under cash basis accounting, revenue is recorded only when cash is received, and expenses are recorded only when paid.
- Generally accepted accounting principles require accrual basis accounting because the cash basis often causes misleading financial statements.

STUDY OBJECTIVE 9

Prepare adjusting entries for the alternative treatment of prepayments.

ALTERNATIVE TREATMENT

- Some businesses use an alternative treatment for prepaids and unearned revenues.
- Instead of debiting an asset at the time an expense is prepaid, the amount is charged to an expense account.
- Instead of crediting a liability at the time cash is received in advance of earning it, the amount is credited to a revenue account.
- This treatment of prepaid expenses and unearned revenues will ultimately result in the same effect on the financial statements as initial entries to balance sheet accounts and then adjusting entries.

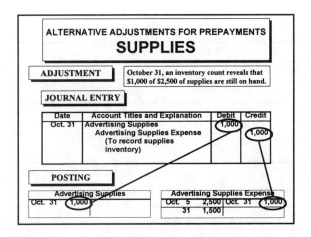

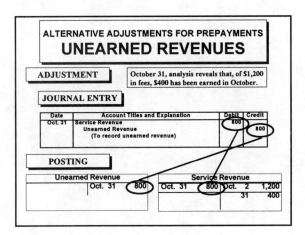

ILLUSTRATION 3A-7
SUMMARY OF BASIC RELATIONSHIPS FOR PREPAYMENTS

Type of Adjustment	Account Relationship	Reason for Adjustment	Account Balances before Adjustment	Adjusting Entry
1 Prepaid Expenses	Assets and Expenses	a Prepaid expenses initially recorded in asset accounts have been used.	Assets overstated Expenses understated	Dr Expenses Cr Assets
		b Prepaid expenses initially recorded in expense accounts have not been used.	Assets understated Expenses overstated	Dr Assets Cr Expenses
2 Unearned Revenues	Liabilities and Revenues	a Unearned revenues initially recorded in liability accounts have been earned.	Liabilities overstated Revenues understated	Dr Liabilities Cr Revenues
		b Unearned revenues initially recorded in revenue accounts have not been earned.	Liabilities understated Revenues understated	Dr Revenues Cr Liabilities

CHAPTER 3
ADJUSTING THE ACCOUNTS

Chapter 4
Completion of the Accounting Cycle

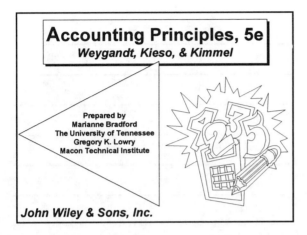

Accounting Principles, 5e
Weygandt, Kieso, & Kimmel

Prepared by
Marianne Bradford
The University of Tennessee
Gregory K. Lowry
Macon Technical Institute

John Wiley & Sons, Inc.

CHAPTER 4
COMPLETION OF THE ACCOUNTING CYCLE

After studying this chapter, you should be able to:

1 Prepare a work sheet.
2 Explain the process of closing the books.
3 Describe the content and purpose of a post-closing trial balance.
4 State the required steps in the accounting cycle.
5 Explain the approaches to preparing correcting entries.
6 Identify the sections of a classified balance sheet.

PREVIEW OF CHAPTER 4

Completion of the Acccounting Cycle

Using a Work Sheet	Closing the Books
➢ Steps in preparation	➢ Preparing closing entries
➢ Preparing financial statements	➢ Posting closing entries
➢ Preparing adjusting entries	➢ Post-closing trial balance

PREVIEW OF CHAPTER 4

Completion of the Acccounting Cycle

Summary of Accounting Cycle	Classified Financial Statements
➤ Reversing entries (optional)	➤ Standard classification
➤ Correcting entries (avoidable)	➤ Balance sheet illustration

---

STUDY OBJECTIVE 1

Prepare a work sheet.

WORK SHEET

- A work sheet is a multiple-column form that may be used in the adjustment process and in preparing financial statements.
- It is a working tool or a supplementary device for the accountant and not a permanent accounting record.
- Use of a work sheet should make the preparation of adjusting entries and financial statements easier.

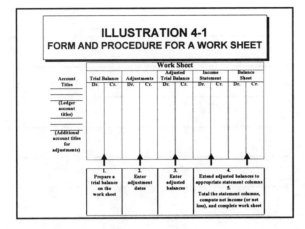

ILLUSTRATION 4-1
FORM AND PROCEDURE FOR A WORK SHEET

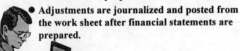

WORK SHEET

- The use of a work sheet is optional.
- When a work sheet is used, financial statements are prepared from the worksheet.
- Adjustments are journalized and posted from the work sheet after financial statements are prepared.

STEPS IN PREPARING A WORKSHEET

1 Prepare a trial balance on the worksheet
2 Enter the adjustments in the adjustments columns
3 Enter adjusted balances in the adjusted trial balance columns
4 Extend adjusted trial balance amounts to appropriate financial statement columns
5 Total the statement columns, compute net income (loss), and complete the worksheet

PREPARING A WORKSHEET
1 PREPARING A TRIAL BALANCE

PIONEER ADVERTISING AGENCY
Work Sheet
For the Month Ended October 31, 1999

Account Titles	Trial Balance Dr.	Trial Balance Cr.	Adjustments Dr.	Adjustments Cr.	Adjusted Trial Balance Dr.	Adjusted Trial Balance Cr.
Cash	15,200					
Advertising Supplies	2,500					
Prepaid Insurance	600					
Office Equipment	5,000					
Notes Payable		5,000				
Accounts Payable		2,500				
Unearned Fees		1,200				
C.R. Byrd, Capital		10,000				
C.R. Byrd, Drawing	500					
Fees Earned		10,000				
Salaries Expense	4,000					
Rent Expense	900					
Totals	28,700	28,700				
Advertising Supplies Expense						
Insurance Expense						
Accum. Depr. — Office Equip.						
Depreciation Expense						
Interest Expense						
Accounts Receivable						
Interest Payable						
Salaries Payable						
Totals						

PREPARING A WORKSHEET
2 ENTER THE ADJUSTMENTS

PIONEER ADVERTISING AGENCY
Work Sheet
For the Month Ended October 31, 1999

Account Titles	Trial Balance Dr.	Trial Balance Cr.	Adjustments Dr.	Adjustments Cr.	Adjusted Trial Balance Dr.	Adjusted Trial Balance Cr.
Cash	15,200					
Advertising Supplies	2,500			a 1,500		
Prepaid Insurance	600			b 50		
Office Equipment	5,000					
Notes Payable		5,000				
Accounts Payable		2,500				
Unearned Fees		1,200	d 400			
C.R. Byrd, Capital		10,000				
C.R. Byrd, Drawing	500					
Fees Earned		10,000		d 400		
				e 200		
Salaries Expense	4,000		g 1,200			
Rent Expense	900					
Totals	28,700	28,700				
Advertising Supplies Expense			a 1,500			
Insurance Expense			b 50			
Accum. Depr. — Office Equip.				c 40		
Depreciation Expense			c 40			
Interest Expense			f 50			
Accounts Receivable			e 200			
Interest Payable				f 50		
Salaries Payable				g 1,200		
Totals			3,440	3,440		

PREPARING A WORKSHEET
3 ENTER ADJUSTED BALANCES

PIONEER ADVERTISING AGENCY
Work Sheet
For the Month Ended October 31, 1999

Account Titles	Trial Balance Dr.	Trial Balance Cr.	Adjustments Dr.	Adjustments Cr.	Adjusted Trial Balance Dr.	Adjusted Trial Balance Cr.
Cash	15,200				15,200	
Advertising Supplies	2,500			a 1,500	1,000	
Prepaid Insurance	600			b 50	550	
Office Equipment	5,000				5,000	
Notes Payable		5,000				5,000
Accounts Payable		2,500				2,500
Unearned Fees		1,200	d 400			800
C.R. Byrd, Capital		10,000				10,000
C.R. Byrd, Drawing	500				500	
Fees Earned		10,000		d 400		10,600
				e 200		
Salaries Expense	4,000		g 1,200		5,200	
Rent Expense	900				900	
Totals	28,700	28,700				
Advertising Supplies Expense			a 1,500		1,500	
Insurance Expense			b 50		50	
Accum. Depr. — Office Equip.				c 40		40
Depreciation Expense			c 40		40	
Interest Expense			f 50		50	
Accounts Receivable			e 200		200	
Interest Payable				f 50		50
Salaries Payable				g 1,200		1,200
Totals			3,440	3,440	30,190	30,190

PREPARING A WORKSHEET
4 EXTEND ADJUSTED BALANCES

PIONEER ADVERTISING AGENCY
Work Sheet
For the Month Ended October 31, 1999

Account Titles	Adjusted Trial Balance Dr.	Cr.	Income Statement Dr.	Cr.	Balance Sheet Dr.	Cr.
Cash	15,200					
Advertising Supplies	1,000					
Prepaid Insurance	550					
Office Equipment	5,000					
Notes Payable		5,000				
Accounts Payable		2,500				
Unearned Fees		800				
C.R. Byrd, Capital		10,000				
C.R. Byrd, Drawing	500					
Fees Earned		10,600		10,600		
Salaries Expense	5,200		5,200			
Rent Expense	900		900			
Advertising Supplies Expense	1,500		1,500			
Insurance Expense	50		50			
Accum. Depr. — Office Equip.		40				
Depreciation Expense	40		40			
Interest Expense	50		50			
Accounts Receivable	200					
Interest Payable		50				
Salaries Payable		1,200				
Totals	30,190	30,190	7,740	10,600	22,450	19,590
Net Income			2,860			2,860
Totals			10,600	10,600	22,450	22,450

PREPARING A WORKSHEET
4 EXTEND ADJUSTED BALANCES

PIONEER ADVERTISING AGENCY
Work Sheet
For the Month Ended October 31, 1999

Account Titles	Adjusted Trial Balance Dr.	Cr.	Income Statement Dr.	Cr.	Balance Sheet Dr.	Cr.
Cash	15,200				15,200	
Advertising Supplies	1,000				1,000	
Prepaid Insurance	550				550	
Office Equipment	5,000				5,000	
Notes Payable		5,000				5,000
Accounts Payable		2,500				2,500
Unearned Fees		800				800
C.R. Byrd, Capital		10,000				10,000
C.R. Byrd, Drawing	500				500	
Fees Earned		10,600		10,600		
Salaries Expense	5,200		5,200			
Rent Expense	900		900			
Advertising Supplies Expense	1,500		1,500			
Insurance Expense	50		50			
Accum. Depr. — Office Equip.		40				40
Depreciation Expense	40		40			
Interest Expense	50		50			
Accounts Receivable	200				200	
Interest Payable		50				50
Salaries Payable		1,200				1,200
Totals	30,190	30,190	7,740	10,600	22,450	19,590
Net Income			2,860			2,860
Totals			10,600	10,600	22,450	22,450

ADJUSTING ENTRIES
JOURNALIZED

GENERAL JOURNAL

Date	Account Titles and Explanation	Ref.	Debit	Credit
1999	a			
Oct. 31	Advertising Supplies Expense		1,500	
	Advertising Supplies			1,500
	b			
31	Insurance Expense		50	
	Prepaid Insurance			50
	c			
31	Depreciation Expense		40	
	Accumulated Depreciation - Office Equipment			40
	d			
31	Unearned Fees		400	
	Fees Earned			400
	e			
31	Accounts Receivable		200	
	Fees Earned			200
	f			
31	Interest Expense		50	
	Interest Payable			50
	g			
31	Salaries Expense		1,200	
	Salaries Payable			1,200

Slide 1

PREPARATION OF FINANCIAL STATEMENTS
INCOME STATEMENT

PIONEER ADVERTISING AGENCY
Income Statement
For the Month Ended October 31, 1999

Revenues		
Service revenue		$ 10,600
Expenses		
Salaries expense	$ 5,200	
Advertising supplies expense	1,500	
Rent expense	900	
Insurance expense	50	
Interest expense	50	
Depreciation expense	40	
Total expenses		7,740
Net income		$ 2,860

> The income statement is prepared from the income statement columns of the work sheet.

Slide 2

PREPARATION OF FINANCIAL STATEMENTS
OWNER'S EQUITY STATEMENT

PIONEER ADVERTISING AGENCY
Owner's Equity Statement
For the Month Ended October 31, 1999

C.R. Byrd, Capital, October 1		$ -0-
Add: Investments	$ 10,000	
Net income	2,860	12,860
		12,860
Less: Drawings		500
C.R. Byrd, Capital, October 31		$ 12,360

> The owner's equity statement is prepared from the balance sheet columns of the work sheet.

Slide 3

PREPARATION OF FINANCIAL STATEMENTS
BALANCE SHEET

PIONEER ADVERTISING AGENCY
Balance Sheet
October 31, 1999

Assets			Liabilities and Owner's Equity		
Cash		$ 15,200	Liabilities		
Accounts receivable		200	Notes payable		$ 5,000
Advertising supplies		1,000	Accounts payable		2,500
Prepaid insurance		550	Interest payable		50
Office equipment	$ 5,000		Unearned revenue		800
Less: Accumulated depreciation	40	4,960	Salaries payable		1,200
			Total liabilities		9,550
			Owner's equity		
			C.R. Byrd, Capital		12,360
Total assets		$ 21,910	Total liabilities and owner's equity		$ 21,910

> The balance sheet is prepared from the balance sheet columns of the work sheet.

STUDY OBJECTIVE 2

Explain the process of closing the books.

ILLUSTRATION 4-5
TEMPORARY VERSUS PERMANENT ACCOUNTS

TEMPORARY (NOMINAL) These accounts are closed	PERMANENT (REAL) These accounts are not closed
All revenue accounts	All asset accounts
All expense accounts	All liability accounts
Owner's drawing	Owner's capital account

CLOSING ENTRIES

- Closing entries formally recognize in the ledger the transfer of net income (loss) and owner's drawings to owner's capital.
- Journalizing and posting closing entries is a required step in the accounting cycle.
- A temporary account, Income Summary, is used in closing revenue and expense accounts to minimize the amount of detail in the permanent owner's capital account.

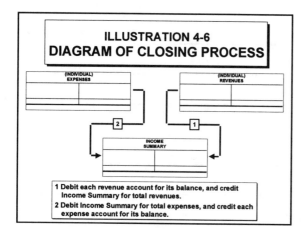

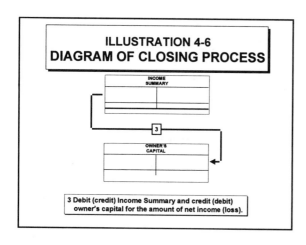

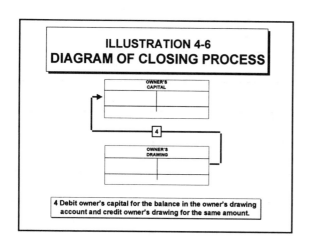

ILLUSTRATION 4-7
CLOSING ENTRIES JOURNALIZED

GENERAL JOURNAL

Date	Account Titles and Explanation	Ref.	Debit	Credit
1999 Oct. 1	Service Revenue	50	10,600	
	Income Summary	49		10,600
	(To close revenue acccount)			

INCOME SUMMARY No. 49

Date	Explanation	Debit	Credit	Balance
1999 Oct. 31			10,600	10,600

SERVICE REVENUE No. 50

Date	Explanation	Debit	Credit	Balance
1999 Oct. 31				10,600
31		10,600		–0–

ILLUSTRATION 4-7
CLOSING ENTRIES JOURNALIZED

GENERAL JOURNAL

Date	Account Titles and Explanation	Ref.	Debit	Credit
1999 Oct. 31	Income Summary	49	7,740	
	Salaries Expense	60		5,200
	Advertising Supplies Expense	61		1,500
	Rent Expense	62		900
	Insurance Expense	63		50
	Interest Expense	64		50
	Depreciation Expense	65		40
	(To close expense accounts)			

INCOME SUMMARY No. 49

Date	Explanation	Debit	Credit	Balance
1999 Oct. 31			10,600	10,600
31		7,740		2,860

ILLUSTRATION 4-7
CLOSING ENTRIES JOURNALIZED

GENERAL JOURNAL

Date	Account Titles and Explanation	Ref.	Debit	Credit
1999 Oct. 31	(3) Income Summary	49	2,860	
	C. R. Byrd, Capital	40		2,860
	(To close net income to capital)			

INCOME SUMMARY No. 49

Date	Explanation	Debit	Credit	Balance
1999 Oct. 31			10,600	10,600
31		7,740		2,860
		2,860		–0–

C. R. BYRD, CAPITAL No. 40

Date	Explanation	Debit	Credit	Balance
1999 Oct. 31			10,000	10,000
31			2,860	12,860

ILLUSTRATION 4-7
CLOSING ENTRIES JOURNALIZED

GENERAL JOURNAL

Date	Account Titles and Explanation	Ref.	Debit	Credit
1999	(4)			
Oct. 31	C. R. Byrd, Capital	40	500	
	C. R. Byrd, Drawing	41		500
	(To close net income to capital)			

C. R. BYRD, DRAWING No. 41

Date	Explanation	Debit	Credit	Balance
1999				
Oct. 31		500		500
31			500	–0–

C. R. BYRD, CAPITAL No. 40

Date	Explanation	Debit	Credit	Balance
1999				
Oct. 31			10,000	10,000
31				12,860
31		500		12,360

CAUTIONS RELATING TO CLOSING ENTRIES

A couple of cautions relating to closing entries:

1 Avoid unintentionally doubling the revenue and expense balances rather than zeroing them.

2 Do not close owner's drawing through the Income Summary account. Owner's drawing is not an expense, and it is not a factor in determining net income.

POSTING CLOSING ENTRIES

- All temporary accounts have zero balances after posting the closing entries.
- The balance in Owner's Capital represents the total equity of the owner at the end of the accounting period.
- No entries are journalized and posted to Owner's Capital during the year.
- As part of the closing process, the temporary accounts (revenues and expenses) are totaled, balanced, and double ruled.
- The permanent accounts (assets, liabilities, and owner's capital) are not closed.

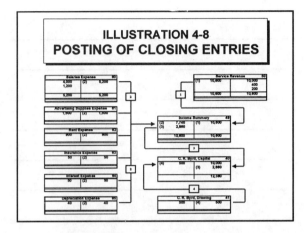

ILLUSTRATION 4-8
POSTING OF CLOSING ENTRIES

STUDY OBJECTIVE 3

Describe the content and purpose
of a post-closing trial balance.

POST-CLOSING
TRIAL BALANCE

● After all closing entries have been
journalized and posted, a post-closing
trial balance is prepared.

● The purpose of this trial balance is to
prove the equality of the permanent
account balances that are carried
forward into the next accounting
period.

ILLUSTRATION 4-9
POST-CLOSING TRIAL BALANCE

PIONEER ADVERTISING AGENCY
Post-Closing Trial Balance
October 31, 1999

		Debit	Credit
Cash		$ 15,200	
Accounts Receivable	The post-closing trial balance is prepared from the permanent accounts in the ledger.	200	
Advertising Supplies		1,000	
Prepaid Insurance		550	
Office Equipment		5,000	
Accumulated Depreciation — Office Equipment			$ 40
Notes Payable			5,000
Accounts Payable	The post-closing trial balance provides evidence that the journalizing and posting of closing entries has been properly completed.		2,500
Interest Payable			50
Unearned Revenue			800
Salaries Payable			1,200
C. R. Byrd, Capital			12,360
		$ 21,950	$ 21,950

STUDY OBJECTIVE 4

State the required steps in the accounting cycle.

STEPS IN THE ACCOUNTING CYCLE

1 Analyze business transactions
2 Journalize the transactions
3 Post to ledger accounts
4 Prepare a trial balance
5 Journalize and post adjusting entries

STEPS IN THE ACCOUNTING CYCLE

6 Prepare an adjusted trial balance

7 Prepare financial statements:
Income statement, Owner's Equity Statement, Balance Sheet

8 Journalize and post closing entries

9 Prepare a post-closing trial balance

_____

_____

_____

_____

_____

_____

REVERSING ENTRIES

- A reversing entry is made at the beginning of the next accounting period.
- The purpose of reversing entries is to simplify the recording of a subsequent transaction related to an adjusting entry.
- Reversing entries are most often used to reverse two types of adjusting entries: accrued revenues and accrued expenses.

_____

_____

_____

_____

_____

_____

ILLUSTRATIVE EXAMPLE OF REVERSING ENTRY

1999	Initial Salary Entry		
Oct. 26	Salaries Expense	4,000	
	Cash		4,000
	(To record Oct. 26 payroll)		
	Adjusting Entry		
31	Salaries Expense	1,200	
	Salaries Payable		1,200
	(To record accrued salaries)		
	Closing Entry		
31	Income Summary	5,200	
	Salaries Expense		5,200
	(To close salaries expense)		
	Reversing Entry		
Nov. 1	Salaries Payable	1,200	
	Salaries Expense		1,200
	(To reverse Oct. 31 adjusting entry)		
	Subsequent Salary Entry		
9	Salaries Expense	4,000	
	Cash		4,000
	(To record Nov. 9 payroll)		

_____

_____

_____

_____

_____

_____

STUDY OBJECTIVE 5

Explain the approaches to preparing correcting entries.

CORRECTING ENTRIES

- Errors that occur in recording transactions should be corrected as soon as they are discovered by preparing correcting entries.
- Correcting entries are unnecessary if the records are free of errors; they can be journalized and posted whenever an error is discovered.
- They involve any combination of balance sheet and income statement accounts

---

ILLUSTRATIVE EXAMPLE OF CORRECTING ENTRY 1

	Incorrect Entry		
May 10	Cash	50	
	Fees Earned		50
	(To record collection from customer an account)		
	Correct Entry		
10	Cash	50	
	Accounts Receivable		50
	(To record collection from customer an account)		
	Correcting Entry		
20	Fees Earned	50	
	Accounts Receivable		50
	(To correct entry of May 10)		

ILLUSTRATIVE EXAMPLE OF CORRECTING ENTRY 2

	Incorrect Entry		
May 18	Delivery Equipment	45	
	Accounts Payable		45
	(To record purchase of equipment on account)		
	Correct Entry		
18	Office Equipment	450	
	Accounts Payable		450
	(To record purchase of equipment on account)		
	Correcting Entry		
June 3	Office Equipment	450	
	Delivery Equipment		45
	Accounts Payable		405
	(To correct entry of May 18)		

STUDY OBJECTIVE 6

Identify the sections of a classified balance sheet.

ILLUSTRATION 4-17
STANDARD BALANCE SHEET CLASSIFICATIONS

- Financial statements become more useful when the elements are classified into significant subgroups.
- A classified balance sheet generally has the following standard classifications:

Assets	Liabilities and Owner's Equity
Current Assets	Current Liabilities
Long-Term Invesments	Long-Term Liabilities
Property, Plant and Equipment	Owner's (Stockholders') Equity
Intangible Assets	

CURRENT ASSETS

- Current assets are cash and other resources that are reasonably expected to be realized in cash or sold or consumed in the business within one year of the balance sheet date or the company's operating cycle, whichever is longer.
- Current assets are listed in the order of their liquidity.
- The operating cycle of a company is the average time that is required to go from cash to cash in producing revenues.
- Examples of current assets are inventory, accounts receivable and cash.

LONG-TERM INVESTMENTS

- Long-term investments are resources that can be realized in cash, but the conversion into cash in not expected within one year or the operating cycle, whichever is longer.
- Examples include investments in bonds of another company or investment in land held for resale.

PROPERTY, PLANT, AND EQUIPMENT

- Tangible resources of a relatively permanent nature that are used in the business and not intended for sale are classified as property, plant, and equipment.
- Examples include land, buildings and machinery.

INTANGIBLE ASSETS

- Intangible assets are noncurrent resources that do not have physical substance.
- Examples include patents, copyrights, trademarks, or trade names that give the holder exclusive right of used for a specified period of time.

CURRENT LIABILITIES

- Current liabilities are obligations that are reasonably expected to be paid from existing current assets or through the creation of other current liabilities within one year or the operating cycle, whichever is longer.
- Examples include accounts payable, wages payable, interest payable, and current maturities of long-term debt.

LONG-TERM LIABILITIES

- Obligations expected to be paid after one year are classified as long-term liabilities.
- Examples include long-term notes payable, bonds payable, mortgages payable, and lease liabilities.

OWNER'S EQUITY

- The content of the owner's equity section varies with the form of business organization.
- In a proprietorship, there is a single owner's equity account called (Owner's Name), Capital.
- In a partnership, there are separate capital accounts for each partner.
- For a corporation, owners' equity is called stockholders' equity, and it consists of two accounts: Capital Stock and Retained Earnings.

ILLUSTRATION 4-25
CLASSIFIED BALANCE SHEET IN REPORT FORM

PIONEER ADVERTISING AGENCY
Balance Sheet
October 31, 1999

Assets

Current assets		
Cash		$ 15,200
Accounts receivable		200
Advertising supplies		1,000
Prepaid insurance		550
Total current assets		16,950
Property, plant, and equipment		
Office equipment	$ 5,000	
Less: Accumulated depreciation	40	4,960
Total assets		$ 21,910

A classified balance sheet helps the financial statement user determine 1 the availability of assets to meet debts as they come due and 2 the claims of short- and long-term creditors on total assets.

ILLUSTRATION 4-25
CLASSIFIED BALANCE SHEET IN REPORT FORM

Liabilities and Owner's Equity

Current liabilities		
Notes payable		$ 1,000
Accounts payable		2,500
Interest payable		50
Unearned revenue		800
Salaries payable		1,200
Total current liabilities		5,550
Long-term liabilities		
Notes payable		4,000
Total liabilities		9,550
Owner's equity		
C. R. Byrd, Capital		12,360
Total liabilities and owner's equity		$ 21,910

The balance sheet is most often presented in the report form, with the assets shown above the liabilities and owner's equity.

Chapter 5
Accounting for Merchandising Operations

Accounting Principles, 5e
Weygandt, Kieso, & Kimmel

Prepared by
Marianne Bradford
The University of Tennessee
Gregory K. Lowry
Macon Technical Institute

John Wiley & Sons, Inc.

CHAPTER 5
ACCOUNTING FOR MERCHANDISING OPERATIONS

After studying this chapter, you should be able to:

1 Identify the differences between a service enterprise and a merchandising company.

2 Explain the entries for purchases under a perpetual inventory system.

3 Explain the entries for sales revenues under a perpetual inventory system.

4 Explain the computation and importance of gross profit.

CHAPTER 5
ACCOUNTING FOR MERCHANDISING OPERATIONS

After studying this chapter, you should be able to:

5 Identify the features of the income statement for a merchandising company.

6 Explain the steps in the accounting cycle for a merchandising company.

7 Distinguish between a multiple-step and a single-step income statement.

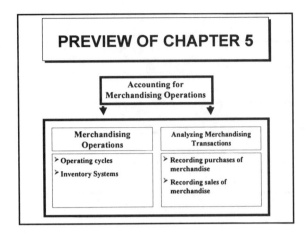

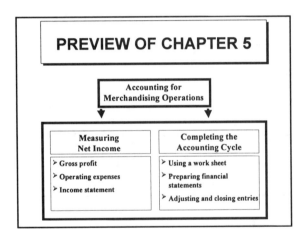

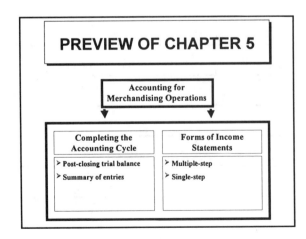

STUDY OBJECTIVE 1

Identify the differences between a service enterprise and a merchandising company.

MERCHANDISING COMPANY

- A merchandising company is an enterprise that buys and sells goods to earn a profit.
  1 Wholesalers sell to retailers
  2 Retailers sell to consumers

VISA

- A merchandiser's primary source of revenue is sales.

MEASURING NET INCOME

- Expenses for a merchandising company are divided into two groups:
  1 cost of goods sold and
  2 operating expenses
- Cost of goods sold is the total cost of merchandise sold during the period.
- Operating expenses are expenses incurred in the process of earning sales revenue. Examples are sales salaries and insurance expense.
- Gross profit is equal to Sales Revenue less Cost of Goods Sold.

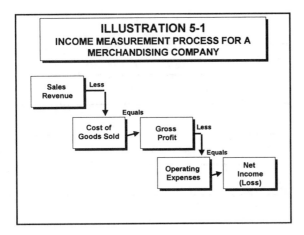

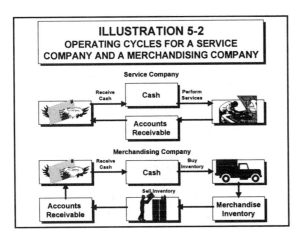

INVENTORY SYSTEMS

Merchandising entities may use either of the following inventory systems:

1 Perpetual

Detailed records of the cost of each item are maintained, and the cost of each item sold is determined from records when the sale occurs.

2 Periodic

Cost of goods sold is determined only at the end of an accounting period.

COST OF GOODS SOLD

- The cost of goods sold may be determined each time a sale occurs or at the end of an accounting period.
- To make the determination when the sale occurs, a company uses a perpetual inventory system.
- When the cost of goods sold is determined only at the end of an accounting period, a company is said to be using a periodic inventory system.

COST OF GOODS SOLD

To determine the cost of goods sold under a periodic inventory system, it is necessary to:

1 record purchases of merchandise,

2 determine the cost of goods purchased, and

3 determine the cost of goods on hand at the beginning and end of the accounting period.

STUDY OBJECTIVE 2

Explain the entries for purchases under a perpetual inventory system.

PURCHASES OF MERCHANDISE

- When merchandise is purchased for resale to customers, the account, Merchandise Inventory, is debited for the cost of goods.
- Like sales, purchases may be made for cash or on account (credit).
- The purchase is normally recorded by the purchaser when the goods are received from the seller.
- Each credit purchase should be supported by a purchase invoice.

PURCHASES OF MERCHANDISE

GENERAL JOURNAL

Date	Account Titles and Explanation	Dr.	Cr.
May 4	Merchandise Inventory	3,800	
	Accounts Payable		3,800
	(To record goods purchased on account, terms 2/10, n/30, from Highpoint Electronic)		

For purchases on account, Merchandise Inventory is debited and Accounts Payable is credited.

PURCHASE RETURNS AND ALLOWANCES

- A purchaser may be dissatisfied with merchandise received because the goods
  1 are damaged or defective,
  2 of inferior quality, or
  3 not in accord with the purchaser's specifications.
- The purchaser initiates the request for a reduction of the balance due through the issuance of a debit memorandum.
- The debit memorandum is a document issued by a buyer to inform a seller that the seller's account has been debited because of unsatisfactory merchandise.

PURCHASE RETURNS AND ALLOWANCES

GENERAL JOURNAL			
Date	Account Titles and Explanation	Dr.	Cr.
May 8	Accounts Payable	300	
	Merchandise Inventory		300
	(To record return of inoperable goods received from Highpoint Electronic, DM No. 126)		

For purchases returns and allowances, Accounts Payable is debited and Merchandise Inventory is credited.

PURCHASE DISCOUNTS

- Credit terms may permit the buyer to claim a cash discount for the prompt payment of a balance due.
- The buyer calls this discount a purchase discount.
- Like a sales discount, a purchase discount is based on the invoice cost less returns and allowances, if any.

PURCHASE DISCOUNTS

GENERAL JOURNAL			
Date	Account Titles and Explanation	Dr.	Cr.
May 14	Accounts Payable	3,500	
	Cash		3,430
	Merchandise Inventory		70
	(To record payment within discount period)		

If payment is made within the discount period, Accounts Payable is debited, Cash is credited, and Merchandise inventory is credited for the discount taken.

PURCHASE DISCOUNTS

GENERAL JOURNAL

Date	Account Titles and Explanation	Debit	Credit
June 3	Accounts Payable	3,500	
	Cash		3,500
	(To record payment with no discount taken)		

If payment is made after the discount period, Accounts Payable is debited and Cash is credited for the full amount.

SAVINGS OBTAINED BY TAKING PURCHASE DISCOUNT

A buyer should usually take all available discounts.

If Chelsea Video takes the discount, it pays $70 less in cash.

If it forgoes the discount and invests the $3,500 for 20 days at 10% interest, it will earn only $19.06 in interest.

The savings obtained by taking the discount is calculated as follows:

Discount of 2% on $3,500	$ 70.00
Interest received on $3,430 (for 20days at 10%)	(19.06)
Savings by taking the discount	$ 50.94

FREE ON BOARD

- The sales agreement should indicate whether the seller or the buyer is to pay the cost of transporting the goods to the buyer's place of business.
- FOB Shipping Point
  1 Goods placed free on board the carrier by seller
  2 Buyer pays freight costs
- FOB Destination
  1 Goods placed free on board at buyer's business
  2 Seller pays freight costs

ACCOUNTING FOR FREIGHT COSTS

- Merchandise Inventory is debited if buyer pays freight.
- Freight-out (or Delivery Expense) is debited if seller pays freight.

ACCOUNTING FOR FREIGHT COSTS

GENERAL JOURNAL

Date	Account Titles and Explanation	Dr.	Cr.
May 6	Merchandise Inventory	150	
	Cash		150
	(To record payment of freight, terms FOB shipping point)		

When the purchaser directly incurs the freight costs, the account Merchandise Inventory is debited and Cash is credited.

ACCOUNTING FOR FREIGHT COSTS

GENERAL JOURNAL

Date	Account Titles and Explanation	Dr.	Cr.
May 4	Freight-out (Delivery Expense)	150	
	Cash		150
	(To record payment of freight on goods sold FOB destination)		

Freight costs incurred by the seller on outgoing merchandise are debited to Freight-out (or Delivery Expense) and Cash is credited.

STUDY OBJECTIVE 3

Explain the entries for sales revenues under a perpetual inventory system.

SALES TRANSACTIONS

- Revenues are reported when earned in accordance with the revenue recognition principle, and in a merchandising company, revenues are earned when the goods are transferred from seller to buyer.
- All sales should be supported by a document such as a cash register tape or sales invoice.

RECORDING CASH SALES

GENERAL JOURNAL			
Date	Account Titles and Explanation	Dr.	Cr.
May 4	Cash	2,200	
	Sales		2,200
	(To record daily cash sales)		
4	Cost of Goods Sold	1,400	
	Merchandise Inventory		1,400
	(To record cost of merchandise sold for cash)		

- For cash sales, Cash is debited and Sales is credited.
- For the cost of goods sold for cash, Cost of Goods Sold is debited and Merchandise Inventory is credited.

RECORDING CREDIT SALES

GENERAL JOURNAL

Date	Account Titles and Explanation	Dr.	Cr.
May 4	Accounts Receivable	3,800	
	Sales		3,800
	(To record credit sales to Chelsea Video per invoice #731)		
4	Cost of Goods Sold	2,400	
	Merchandise Inventory		2,400
	(To record cost of merchandise sold on invoice #731 to Chelsea Video)		

- For credit sales, Accounts Receivable is debited and Sales is credited.
- For the cost of goods sold on account, Cost of Goods Sold is debited and Merchandise Inventory is credited.

SALES RETURNS AND ALLOWANCES

- Sales Returns result when customers are dissatisfied with merchandise and are allowed to return the goods to the seller for credit or a refund.
- Sales Allowances result when customers are dissatisfied, and the seller allows a deduction from the selling price.

SALES RETURNS AND ALLOWANCES

- To grant the return or allowance, the seller prepares a credit memorandum to inform the customer that a credit has been made to the customer's account receivable.
- Sales Returns and Allowances is a contra revenue account to the Sales account.
- The normal balance of Sales Returns and Allowances is a debit.

RECORDING SALES RETURNS AND ALLOWANCES

GENERAL JOURNAL

Date	Account Titles and Explanation	Dr.	Cr.
May 8	Sales Returns and Allowances	300	
	Accounts Receivable		300
	(To record return of inoperable goods delivered to Chelsea Video, per credit memorandum)		
8	Merchandise Inventory	140	
	Cost of Goods Sold		140
	(To record cost of goods returned per credit memorandum)		

● The seller's entry to record a credit memorandum involves a debit to the Sales Returns and Allowances account and a credit to Accounts Receivable. The entry to record the cost of the returned goods involves a debit to Merchandise Inventory and a credit to Cost Goods Sold.

SALES DISCOUNTS

● A sales discount is the offer of a cash discount to a customer for the prompt payment of a balance due.

● Example: If a credit sale has the terms 3/10, n/30, a 3% discount is allowed if payment is made within 10 days. After 10 days there is no discount, and the balance is due in 30 days.

● Sales Discounts is a contra revenue account with a normal debit balance.

CREDIT TERMS

● Credit terms specify the amount and time period for the cash discount.

● They also indicate the length of time in which the purchaser is expected to pay the full invoice price.

TERMS	EXPLANATION
2/10, n/30	A 2% discount may be taken if payment is made within 10 days of the invoice data.
1/10 EOM	A 1% discount is available if payment is made by the 10th of the next month.

RECORDING SALES DISCOUNTS

GENERAL JOURNAL

Date	Account Titles and Explanation	Dr.	Cr.
May 14	Cash	3,430	
	Sales Discounts	70	
	Accounts Receivable		3,500
	(To record collection within 2/10, n/30 discount period from Chelsea Video)		

When cash discounts are taken by customers, the seller debits Sales Discounts.

STUDY OBJECTIVE 4

Explain the computation and importance of gross profit.

ILLUSTRATION 5-8
COMPUTATION OF GROSS PROFIT

Gross profit is determined as follows:

Net sales	$ 460,000
Cost of goods sold	316,000
Gross profit	$ 144,000

ILLUSTRATION 5-9
OPERATING EXPENSES IN COMPUTING NET INCOME

Net income is determined as follows:

Gross profit	$ 144,000
Operating expenses	114,000
Net income	$ 30,000

STUDY OBJECTIVE 5

Identify the features of the income statement for a merchandising company.

ILLUSTRATION 5-10
INCOME STATEMENT FOR A MERCHANDISING COMPANY

HIGHPOINT ELECTRONIC
Income Statement
For the Year Ended December 31, 1999

Sales revenues			
Sales			$ 480,000
Less: Sales returns and allowances		$ 12,000	
Sales discounts		8,000	20,000
Net sales			460,000
Cost of goods sold			316,000
Gross profit			144,000
Operating expenses			
Store salaries expense		45,000	
Rent expense		19,000	
Utilities expense		17,000	
Advertising expense		16,000	
Depreciation expense — store equipment		8,000	
Freight-out		7,000	
Insurance expense		2,000	
Total operating expenses			114,000
Net income			$ 30,000

The income statement for retailers and wholesalers contains the following three features not found in the income statement of a service enterprise:
1 a sales revenue section,
2 a cost of goods sold section, and
3 gross profit.

STUDY OBJECTIVE 6

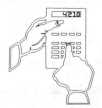

Explain the steps in the accounting cycle for a merchandising company.

ILLUSTRATION 5-11
WORK SHEET FOR A MERCHANDISING COMPANY

HIGHPOINT ELECTRONIC
Work Sheet
For the Year Ended December 31, 1999

Account Titles	Trial Balance Dr.	Trial Balance Cr.	Adjustments Dr.	Adjustments Cr.	Adjusted Trial Balance Dr.	Adjusted Trial Balance Cr.
Cash	9,500				9,500	
Accounts Receivable	16,100				16,100	
Merchandise Inventory	40,000				40,000	
Prepaid Insurance	3,800			a 2,000	1,800	
Store Equipment	80,000				80,000	
Accumulated Depreciation		16,000		b 8,000		24,000
Accounts Payable		20,400				20,400
R.A. Lamb, Capital		83,000				83,000
R.A. Lamb, Drawing	15,000				15,000	
Sales		480,000				480,000
Sales Returns and Allowances	12,000				12,000	
Sales Discounts	8,000				8,000	
Cost of Goods Sold	316,000				316,000	
Freight-out	7,000				7,000	
Advertising Expense	16,000				16,000	
Rent Expense	19,000				19,000	
Store Salaries Expense	40,000		c 5,000		45,000	
Utilities Expense	17,000				17,000	
Totals	599,400	599,400				
Insurance Expense			a 2,000		2,000	
Depreciation Expense			b 8,000		8,000	
Salaries Payable				c 5,000		5,000
Totals			15,000	15,000	612,400	612,400

USING A WORK SHEET

Trial Balance Columns

1 Data from the trial balance are obtained from the ledger balances of Highpoint Electronic at December 31.

2 The amount shown for Merchandise Inventory, $40,000, is the year-end inventory amount which results from the application of a perpetual inventory system.

USING A WORK SHEET

Adjustments Columns

1 A merchandising company usually has the same types of adjustments as a service company.

2 Work sheet adjustments a, b, and c are for insurance, depreciation, and salaries.

Adjusted Trial Balance - The adjusted trial balance shows the balance of all accounts after adjustment at the end of the accounting period.

ILLUSTRATION 5-11
WORK SHEET FOR A
MERCHANDISING COMPANY

HIGHPOINT ELECTRONIC
Work Sheet
For the Year Ended December 31, 1999

Account Titles	Adjusted Trial Balance Dr.	Adjusted Trial Balance Cr.	Income Statement Dr.	Income Statement Cr.	Balance Sheet Dr.	Balance Sheet Cr.
Cash	9,500				9,500	
Accounts Receivable	16,100				16,100	
Merchandise Inventory	40,000				40,000	
Prepaid Insurance	1,800				1,800	
Store Equipment	80,000				80,000	
Accumulated Depreciation		24,000				24,000
Accounts Payable		20,400				20,400
R.A. Lamb, Capital		83,000				83,000
R.A. Lamb, Drawing	15,000				15,000	
Sales		480,000		480,000		
Sales Returns and Allowances	12,000		12,000			
Sales Discounts	8,000		8,000			
Cost of Goods Sold	316,000		316,000			
Freight-out	7,000		7,000			
Advertising Expense	16,000		16,000			
Rent Expense	19,000		19,000			
Store Salaries Expense	45,000		45,000			
Utilities Expense	17,000		17,000			
Totals						
Insurance Expense	2,000		2,000			
Depreciation Expense	8,000		8,000			
Salaries Payable		5,000				5,000
Totals	612,400	612,400	450,000	480,000	162,400	132,400
Net Income			30,000			30,000
Totals			480,000	480,000	162,400	162,400

USING A WORK SHEET

Income Statement Columns

1 The accounts and balances that affect the income statement are transferred from the adjusted trial balance columns to the income statement columns for Highpoint Electronic at December 31.

2 All of the amounts in the income statement credit column should be totaled and compared to the total of the amounts in the income statement debit column.

USING A WORK SHEET

Balance Sheet Columns

1 The major difference between the balance sheets of a service company and a merchandising company is inventory.

2 For Highpoint Electronic, the ending Merchandise Inventory amount of $40,000 is shown in the balance sheet debit column.

3 The information to prepare the owner's equity statement is also found in these columns.

ILLUSTRATION 5-12
OWNER'S EQUITY STATEMENT

● Financial statements for a merchandising company are prepared from the financial statement columns of the work sheet.

● The owner's equity statement for Highpoint Electronic is as follows:

HIGHPOINT ELECTRONIC
Owner's Equity Statement
For the Year Ended December 31, 1999

R.A. Lamb, Capital, January 1	$ 83,000
Add: Net income	30,000
	113,000
Less: Drawings	15,000
R.A. Lamb, Capital, December 31	$ 98,000

ILLUSTRATION 5-13
CLASSIFIED BALANCE SHEET

HIGHPOINT ELECTRONIC
Balance Sheet
October 31, 1999

Assets

Current assets		
Cash		$ 9,500
Accounts receivable		16,100
Merchandise inventory		40,000
Prepaid insurance		1,800
Total current assets		67,400
Property, plant, and equipment		
Store equipment	$ 80,000	
Less: Accumulated depreciation — store equipment	24,000	56,000
Total assets		$ 123,400

In the balance sheet, merchandise inventory is reported as a current asset immediately below accounts receivable. This is because items are listed under current assets in the order of liquidity.

Liabilities and Owner's Equity

Current liabilities	
Accounts payable	$ 20,400
Salaries payable	5,000
Total current liabilities	25,400
Owner's equity	
R. A. Byrd, Capital	98,000
Total liabilities and owner's equity	$ 123,400

CLOSING ENTRIES

- Adjusting entries are journalized from the adjustment columns of the work sheet.
- All accounts that affect the determination of net income are closed to Income Summary.
- Data for the preparation of closing entries may be obtained from the income statement columns of the work sheet.

GENERAL JOURNAL

Date	Account Titles and Explanation	Debit	Credit
1999	(1)		
Dec. 31	Sales	480,000	
	Income Summary		480,000
	(To close income statement accounts		
	with credit balances)		

CLOSING ENTRIES

Cost of Goods Sold is a new account that must be closed to Income Summary.

GENERAL JOURNAL

Date	Account Titles and Explanation	Debit	Credit
1999	(2)		
Dec. 31	Income Summary	450,000	
	Sales Returns and Allowances		12,000
	Sales Discounts		8,000
	Cost of goods sold		316,000
	Store Salaries Expense		45,000
	Rent Expense		19,000
	Freight-out		7,000
	Advertising Expense		16,000
	Utilities Expense		17,000
	Depreciation Expense		8,000
	Insurance Expense		2,000
	(To close income statement accounts		
	with debit balances)		

CLOSING ENTRIES

GENERAL JOURNAL

Date	Account Titles and Explanation	Debit	Credit
1999	(3)		
Dec. 31	Income Summary	30,000	
	R. A. Lamb, Capital		30,000
	(To close net income to capital)		
	(4)		
31	R. A. Lamb, Capital	15,000	
	R. A. Lamb, Drawing		15,000
	(To close drawings to capital)		

- After the closing entries are posted, all temporary accounts have zero balances.
- It addition, R. A. Lamb, Capital has a credit balance of $98,000 ($83,000 + $30,000 - $15,000).

ILLUSTRATION 5-14
POST-CLOSING TRIAL BALANCE

HIGHPOINT ELECTRONIC
Post-Closing Trial Balance
December 31, 1999

		Debit	Credit
Cash		$ 9,500	
Accounts receivable	After the closing entries	16,100	
Merchandise inventory	are posted, the	40,000	
Prepaid insurance	post-closing trial	1,800	
Store equipment	balance is prepared.	80,000	
Accumulated depreciation	The only new account in		$ 24,000
Accounts payable	the post-closing trial		20,400
Salaries payable	balance is Merchandise		5,000
R. A. Lamb, capital	Inventory.		98,000
		$ 147,400	$ 147,400

STUDY OBJECTIVE 7

Distinguish between a multiple-step and a single-step income statement.

MULTIPLE-STEP
INCOME STATEMENT

● Includes sales revenue, cost of goods sold and gross profit sections

● Additional nonoperating sections may be added for:

1 Revenues and expenses resulting from secondary or auxiliary operations

2 Gains and losses unrelated to operations

MULTIPLE-STEP INCOME STATEMENT

Nonoperating sections are reported after income from operations and are classified as:

1 Other revenues and gains

2 Other expenses and losses

3 Operating expenses may be subdivided into:

   a Selling Expenses

   b Administrative Expenses

ILLUSTRATION 5-18
SINGLE-STEP INCOME STATEMENT

HIGHPOINT ELECTRONIC
Income Statement
For the Year Ended December 31, 1999

Revenues		
Net sales	All data are classified under two categories:	$ 460,000
Interest revenue		3,000
Gain on sale of equipment	1 Revenues	600
Total revenues	2 Expenses	463,600
Expenses	Only one step is required in determining net income or net loss.	
Cost of goods sold		$ 316,000
Selling expenses		76,000
Administrative expenses		38,000
Interest expense		1,800
Casualty loss from vandalism		200
Total expenses		432,000
Net income		$ 31,600

CHAPTER 5
ACCOUNTING FOR MERCHANDISING OPERATIONS

WILEY
Publishers Since 1807

Accounting Principles, 5e
Weygandt, Kieso, & Kimmel

Prepared by
Marianne Bradford
The University of Tennessee
Gregory K. Lowry
Macon Technical Institute

John Wiley & Sons, Inc.

CHAPTER 6
ACCOUNTING INFORMATION SYSTEMS

After studying this chapter, you should be able to:

1 Identify the basic principles of accounting information systems.

2 Explain the major phases involved in the development of an accounting system.

3 Describe the nature and purpose of a subsidiary ledger.

4 Explain how special journals are used in journalizing.

5 Indicate how a columnar journal is posted.

6 Distinguish between computer hardware and accounting software and the principal methods of data processing.

7 Identify the key points in comparing manual and electronic accounting systems.

PREVIEW OF CHAPTER 6

Accounting Information Systems

Basic Concepts	Manual Accounting Systems	Electronic Accounting Systems
› Principles of accounting information systems › Developing an accounting system	› Subsidiary ledgers › Subsidiary journals	› Computer hardware › Accounting software › Data processing methods › Comparing manual and electronic systems › A look to the future

STUDY OBJECTIVE 1

Identify the basic principles of accounting information systems.

ACCOUNTING INFORMATION SYSTEMS

- An accounting information system involves collecting and processing data and disseminating financial information to interested parties.

- An AIS may either be manual or computerized.

ILLUSTRATION 6-1
PRINCIPLES OF AN EFFICIENT AND EFFECTIVE ACCOUNTING INFORMATION SYSTEM

Cost Awareness

Costs   Benefits

The accounting system must be cost effective.

Benefits of information must outweigh the cost of providing it.

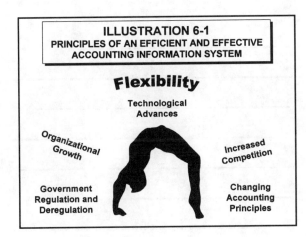

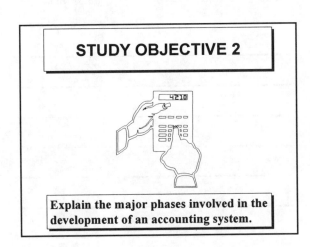

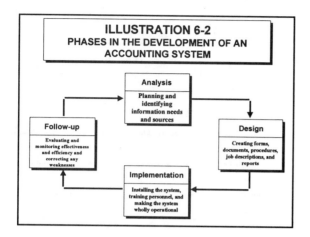

**ILLUSTRATION 6-2
PHASES IN THE DEVELOPMENT OF AN
ACCOUNTING SYSTEM**

MANUAL ACCOUNTING SYSTEMS

- In a manual accounting system, each of the steps in the accounting cycle is performed by hand.
- This means that transactions are entered into a journal and then posted to the ledger.
- Financial statements are thus derived from many manual computations from ledger balances.
- So.....why study manual systems if the real world uses computerized systems?

MANUAL ACCOUNTING SYSTEMS

- Small businesses still abound and most of them begin operations with manual accounting systems and convert to computerized systems as business grows.
- To understand what computerized accounting systems do, one must understand how manual accounting systems work.

STUDY OBJECTIVE 3

Describe the nature and purpose of a subsidiary ledger.

SUBSIDIARY LEDGERS

- A subsidiary ledger is a group of accounts with a common characteristic, such as customer accounts.
- The subsidiary ledger is assembled together to facilitate the recording process by freeing the general ledger from details concerning individual balances.
- Two common subsidiary ledgers are the Accounts Receivable Ledger and the Accounts Payable Ledger.

CONTROL ACCOUNT

- The general ledger account that summarizes subsidiary ledger data is called a control account.
- Each general ledger control account balance must equal the composite balance of the individual accounts in the subsidiary ledger.

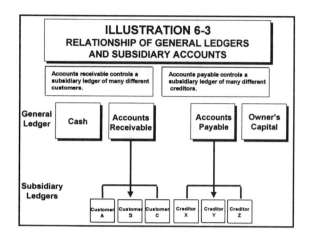

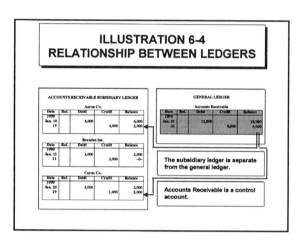

SUBSIDIARY LEDGERS

Advantages of using subsidiary ledgers are that they:

1 Show transactions affecting one customer or one creditor in a single account.

2 Free the general ledger of excessive details.

3 Help locate errors in individual accounts by reducing the number of accounts combined in one ledger and by using controlling accounts.

4 Make possible a division of labor in posting by having one employee post to the general ledger and a different employee post to the subsidiary ledger.

STUDY OBJECTIVE 4

Explain how special journals are used in journalizing.

SPECIAL JOURNALS

- Special journals are used to group similar types of transactions.
- If a transaction cannot be recorded in a special journal, it is recorded in the general journal.
- Special journals permit greater division of labor and reduce time necessary to complete the posting process.

ILLUSTRATION 6-6
USE OF SPECIAL JOURNALS AND THE GENERAL JOURNAL

Sales Journal	Cash Receipts Journal	Purchases Journal	Cash Payments Journal	General Journal
Used for:	Used for:	Used for:	Used for:	Used for:
All sales of merchandise on account	All cash received (including cash sales)	All purchases of merchandise on account	All cash paid (including cash purchases)	Transactions that cannot be entered in a special journal, including correcting, adjusting, and closing entries

The types of special journals used depend largely on the types of transactions that occur frequently in a business enterprise.

ILLUSTRATION 6-7
JOURNALIZING THE SALES JOURNAL
PERPETUAL INVENTORY SYSTEM

KARNS WHOLESALE SUPPLY

SALES JOURNAL 51

Date	Account Debited	Invoice No.	Ref.	Accts. Receivable Dr. Sales Cr.	Cost of Goods Sold Dr. Merchandise Inventory Cr.
1999					
May 3	Abbot Sisters	101		10,600	6,360
7	Babson Co.	102		11,350	7,370
14	Carson Bros.	103		7,800	5,070
19	Deli Co.	104		9,300	6,510
21	Abbot Sisters	105		15,400	10,780
24	Deli Co.	106		21,210	15,900
27	Babson Co.	107		14,570	10,200
				90,230	62,190

- Under a perpetual inventory system, one entry at selling price in the Sales Journal results in a debit to Accounts Receivable and a credit to Sales.
- Another entry at cost results in a debit to Cost of Goods Sold and a credit to Merchandise Inventory.
- Only one line is needed to record each transaction and all entries are made from sales invoices.

ILLUSTRATION 6-9
PROVING THE EQUALITY OF THE POSTINGS
FROM THE SALES JOURNAL

Postings to General Ledger

General Ledger

Credits
Merchandise Inventory	$ 62,190
Sales	90,230
	$ 152,420

Debits
Accounts Receivable	$ 90,230
Cost of Goods Sold	62,190
	$ 152,420

Debit Postings to the Accounts Receivable Subsidiary Ledger

Subsidiary Ledger

Abbot Sisters	$ 26,000
Babson Co.	25,920
Carson Bros.	7,800
Deli Co.	30,510
	$ 90,230

To prove the ledgers it is necessary to determine that 1 the total of the general ledger debit balances equals the total of the general ledger credit balances and 2 the sum of the subsidiary ledger balances equals the balance in the control account.

ADVANTAGES OF A
SALES JOURNAL

1 One-line entry for each sales transaction saves time, because it is not necessary to write out the 4 account titles for each transaction.

2 Only totals, rather than individual entries, are posted to the general ledger, thus saving posting time and reducing the possibilities of errors in posting.

3 A division of labor results, because one individual can take responsibility for the sales journal.

CASH RECEIPTS JOURNAL

KARNS WHOLESALE SUPPLY
Cash Receipts Journal

Date	Accounts Credited	Ref.	Cash Dr.	Sales Discounts Dr.	Accounts Receivable Cr.	Sales Cr.	Other Accounts Cr.
1999							
May 1	D. A. Karns, Capital		6,000				6,000
7			1,900			1,900	
10	Abbot Sisters		10,388	212	10,600		
12			2,600			2,600	
17	Babson Co.		11,123	227	11,350		
22	Notes Payable		6,000				6,000
23	Carson Bros.		7,644	156	7,800		
28	Deli Co.		9,114	186	9,300		
			53,769	781	39,050	4,500	11,000

- Has debit columns for cash and sales discounts and credit columns for accounts receivable, sales, and other accounts
- Posting the cash receipts journal involves posting all column totals once at the end of the month to the appropriate accounts

CASH RECEIPTS JOURNAL

- The total of the Other Accounts column is not posted. The individual amounts comprising the total are posted separately to the general ledger accounts specified in the Accounts Credited column
- The individual amounts in a column are posted daily to the subsidiary ledger account specified in the Accounts Credited column

ILLUSTRATION 6-11
PROVING THE EQUALITY OF
THE CASH RECEIPTS JOURNAL

Debits		Credits	
Cash	$ 53,769	Accounts Receivable	$ 39,050
Sales Discounts	781	Sales	4,500
Cost of goods sold	2,930	Other Accounts	11,000
	$ 57,480	Merchandise Inventory	2,930
			$ 57,480

When the journalizing of a columnar journal has been completed, the amount columns are totaled (footing), and the totals are balanced to prove the equality of the debits and credits (cross-footing).

STUDY OBJECTIVE 5

Indicate how a columnar journal is posted.

ILLUSTRATION 6-12
PROVING THE LEDGERS AFTER POSTING THE SALES AND THE CASH RECEIPTS JOURNALS

Accounts Receivable Subsidiary Ledger	
Abbot Sisters	$ 15,400
Babson Co.	14,570
Deli Co.	21,210
	$ 51,180

General Ledger	
Debits	
Cash	$ 53,769
Accounts Receivable	51,180
Sales Discounts	781
Cost of Goods Sold	65,120
	$ 170,850
Credits	
Notes Payable	$ 6,000
D. A. Karns, Capital	5,000
Sales	94,730
Merchandise Inventory	65,120
	$ 170,850

After the posting of the cash receipts journal is completed, it is necessary to prove the ledgers. The general ledger totals are in agreement and the sum of the subsidiary ledger balances equals the control account balance.

PURCHASES JOURNAL

KARNS WHOLESALE SUPPLY
Purchases Journal

Date	Account Credited	Terms	Ref.	Merchandise Inventory Dr. Accounts Payable Cr.
1999				
May 6	Jasper Manufacturing Inc.	2/10, n/30		11,000
10	Eaton and Howe Inc.	3/10, n/30		7,200
14	Fabor and Son	1/10, n/30		6,900
19	Jasper Manufacturing Inc.	2/10, n/30		17,500
26	Fabor and Son	1/10, n/30		8,700
29	Eaton and Howe Inc.	3/10, n/30		12,600
				63,900

- Each entry results in a debit to Merchandise Inventory and a credit to Accounts Payable
- All entries are made from purchase invoices
- Postings are made daily to the accounts payable subsidiary journal and monthly to the general ledger

ILLUSTRATION 6-15
PROVING THE EQUALITY OF THE PURCHASES JOURNAL

Postings to General Ledger	
Merchandise Inventory (debit)	$ 63,900
Accounts Payable (credit)	$ 63,900

Credit Postings to Accounts Payable Ledger	
Eaton and Howe, Inc.	$ 19,800
Fabor and Son	15,600
Jasper Manufacturing Inc.	28,500
	$ 63,900

To prove the ledgers it is necessary to determine that **1** the total of the general ledger debit balances equals the total of the general ledger credit balances and **2** the sum of the subsidiary ledger balances equals the balance in the control account.

CASH PAYMENTS JOURNAL

KARNS WHOLESALE SUPPLY
Cash Payments Journal

Date	Ck. No.	Accounts Debited	Ref.	Other Accounts Dr.	Accounts Payable Dr.	Merchandise Inventory Cr.	Cash Cr.
1999							
May 1	101	Prepaid Insurance		1,200			1,200
3	102	Freight-in		100			100
8	103	Purchases		400			400
10	104	Jasper Manufacturing Inc.			11,000	220	10,780
19	105	Eaton and Howe Inc.			7,200	216	6,984
23	106	Fabor and Son			6,900	69	6,831
28	107	Jasper Manufacturing Inc.			17,500	350	17,150
30	108	D. A. Karns, Drawing		500			500
				2,200	42,600	855	43,945

- Has multiple columns because of the multiple reasons that cash payments may be made
- Journalizing procedures are similar to cash receipts journal
- All entries are made from prenumbered checks
- Posting procedures are also like the cash receipts journal

EFFECTS ON GENERAL JOURNAL

- Only transactions that cannot be recorded in a special journal are recorded in the general journal.
- When the entry involves both control and subsidiary accounts:
  1 In journalizing, control and subsidiary accounts must be identified
  2 In posting there must be a dual posting (to the control account and subsidiary ledger)

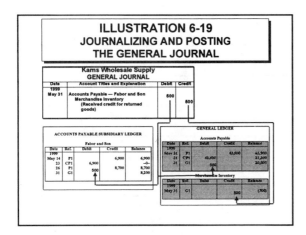

ILLUSTRATION 6-19
JOURNALIZING AND POSTING
THE GENERAL JOURNAL

ELECTRONIC ACCOUNTING SYSTEMS

An electronic accounting system uses computers in processing transaction data and in disseminating accounting information to interested parties.

STUDY OBJECTIVE 6

Distinguish between computer hardware and accounting software and the principal methods of data processing.

COMPUTER HARDWARE

Hardware can be divided into three classes:

1 Mainframes are large powerful very expensive computers that are used to process huge volumes of transactions.

2 Minicomputers are less powerful and not as expensive.

3 Personal computers have speed but less power than minicomputers.

COMPUTER HARDWARE

● Computer hardware is the physical equipment associated with a computerized accounting system.

● The basic hardware configuration of the CPU and peripheral devices.

● The central processing unit (CPU) is composed of three parts:

   1 the control unit,

   2 the internal storage unit, and

   3 the arithmetic-logic unit.

ILLUSTRATION 6-20
COMPUTER HARDWARE

MONITOR

PRINTER   KEYBOARD/MOUSE

Central Processing Unit	Peripheral Equipment
1 Control unit	1 Keyboard/Mouse 2 CD-ROM
2 Computer memory	3 Display screen 4 Printer
	5 Magnetic disk/tape drive

COMPUTER HARDWARE

- A network is two or more linked computers which run on a common software package.
- A computer network may be as small as two computers in the same room.
- The Internet is a worldwide network, with a hookup of more than 40 million computers.

ACCOUNTING SOFTWARE

- Accounting software consists of programs that relate to specific parts of the accounting process.
- Programs exist for general and subsidiary ledgers and for performing steps in the accounting cycle.

- Software can be purchased "off the shelf" or it can be custom-made by individual companies and users.

DATA PROCESSING METHODS

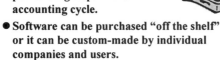

- Refers to how data are entered into and processed by computer
- In batch processing, data is accumulated by classes of transactions and periodically entered into computer and processed in batches.
- In on-line processing files are updated as data entry occurs.

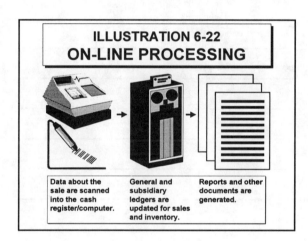

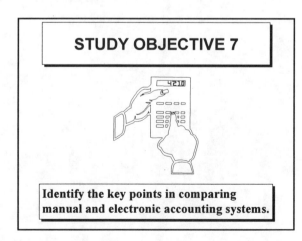

COMPARING MANUAL AND ELECTRONIC SYSTEMS

- Costs and benefits of an electronic system must be evaluated when comparing it to manual systems.
- Costs and benefits to consider are :

  1 dollar costs,

  2 processing speed,

  3 processing errors, and

  4 report generation

CHAPTER 6
ACCOUNTING INFORMATION SYSTEMS

WILEY

Publishers Since 1807

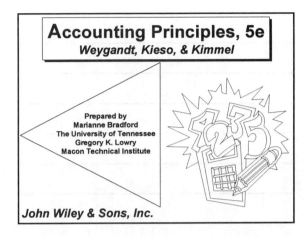

Accounting Principles, 5e
Weygandt, Kieso, & Kimmel

Prepared by
Marianne Bradford
The University of Tennessee
Gregory K. Lowry
Macon Technical Institute

John Wiley & Sons, Inc.

CHAPTER 7
INTERNAL CONTROL AND CASH

After studying this chapter, you should be able to:

1 Define internal control.

2 Identify the principles of internal control.

3 Explain the applications of internal control principles to cash receipts.

4 Describe the applications of internal control principles to cash disbursements.

5 Explain the operation of a petty cash fund.

6 Indicate the control features of a bank account.

7 Prepare a bank reconciliation.

8 Explain the reporting of cash.

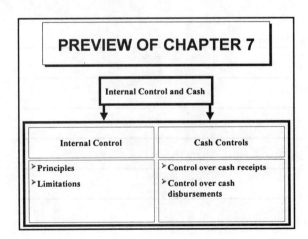

PREVIEW OF CHAPTER 7

Internal Control and Cash

Internal Control	Cash Controls
➢ Principles	➢ Control over cash receipts
➢ Limitations	➢ Control over cash disbursements

PREVIEW OF CHAPTER 7

Internal Control and Cash

Use of a Bank	Reporting Cash
➢ Making deposits	
➢ Writing checks	
➢ Bank statements	
➢ Reconciling the bank account	

STUDY OBJECTIVE 1

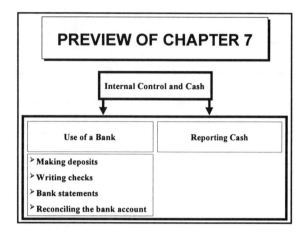

Define internal control.

INTERNAL CONTROL

Internal control consists of the plan of organization and all the related methods and measures adopted within a business in order to:

1 Safeguard its assets

2 enhance the accuracy and reliability of its accounting records

STUDY OBJECTIVE 2

Identify the principles of internal control.

ILLUSTRATION 7-1
PRINCIPLES OF INTERNAL CONTROL

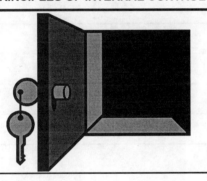

PRINCIPLES OF INTERNAL CONTROL

◆ Establishment of responsibility: control is most effective when only one person is responsible for a given task.

◆ Segregation of duties: the work of one employee should provide a reliable basis for evaluating the work of another employee.

◆ Documentation procedures: documents should provide evidence that transactions and events have occurs.

PRINCIPLES OF INTERNAL CONTROL

◆ Physical, mechanical, and electronic controls: relate primarily to the safeguarding of assets and enhancing accuracy and reliability of the accounting records

◆ Independent internal verification: the review, comparison, and reconciliation of information from two sources.

◆ Other controls: bonding of employees who handle cash, rotating employee's duties, and requiring employees to take vacations.

ILLUSTRATION 7-2 PHYSICAL, MECHANICAL, AND ELECTRONIC CONTROLS

◆ Locked warehouses and storage cabinets for inventories and records

◆ Safes, vaults, and safety deposit boxes for cash and business papers

◆ Time clocks for recording time worked

ILLUSTRATION 7-2 PHYSICAL, MECHANICAL, AND ELECTRONIC CONTROLS

◆ Computer facilities with pass key access

◆ Alarms to prevent break-ins

◆ Television monitors and garment sensors to deter theft

INDEPENDENT INTERNAL VERIFICATION

To obtain maximum benefit from independent internal verification:

1 The verification should be made periodically or on a surprise basis.

2 The verification should be done by an employee who is independent of the personnel responsible for the information.

3 Discrepancies and exceptions should be reported to a management level that can take appropriate correct action.

INDEPENDENT INTERNAL VERIFICATION

◆ Independent internal verification is often assigned to internal auditors.

◆ Internal auditors evaluate the effectiveness of the company's system of internal control on a continuous basis.

◆ Internal auditing is a professional activity within a company, often with direct access to the board of directors.

ILLUSTRATION 7-3
COMPARISON OF SEGREGATION OF DUTIES PRINCIPLE WITH INDEPENDENT INTERNAL VERIFICATION PRINCIPLE

Segregation of Duties

Accounting Employee A
Maintains cash balances per books

Assistant Cashier B
Maintains custody of cash on hand

Independent Internal Verification

Assistant Treasurer A
Makes monthly comparisons: reports any unreconcilable differences to treasurer

LIMITATIONS OF INTERNAL CONTROL

◆ Costs of establishing control procedures should not exceed their expected benefits according to the concept of reasonable assurance.

◆ The human element is also an important factor in every system of internal control. A good system can become ineffective through employee fatigue, carelessness, or indifference.

◆ Collusion may result when two or more individuals work together to get around prescribed controls and may significantly impair the effectiveness of a system.

CASH

◆ Cash includes coins, currency, checks, money orders, and money on hand or on deposit at a bank or similar depository.

◆ Internal control over cash is imperative in order to safeguard cash and assure the accuracy of the accounting records for cash.

STUDY OBJECTIVE 3

Explain the applications of internal control principles to cash receipts.

CONTROL OVER CASH RECEIPTS

◆ Only designated personnel should be authorized to handle or have access to cash receipts.

◆ Different individuals should:

1 receive cash

2 record cash receipt transactions

3 have custody of cash

CONTROL OVER CASH RECEIPTS

◆ Documents should include:

1 remittance advices

2 cash register tapes

3 deposit slips

◆ Cash should be stored in safes and bank vaults

◆ Access to storage areas should be limited to authorized personnel

◆ Cash registers should be used in executing over-the-counter receipts

CONTROL OVER CASH RECEIPTS

◆ Daily cash counts and daily comparisons of total receipts.

◆ All personnel who handle cash receipts should be bonded and required to take vacations.

◆ Control of over-the-counter receipts is centered on cash registers that are visible to customers.

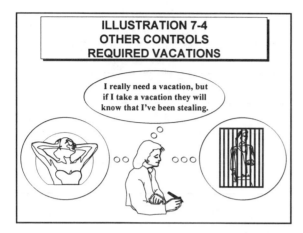

**ILLUSTRATION 7-4
OTHER CONTROLS
REQUIRED VACATIONS**

I really need a vacation, but if I take a vacation they will know that I've been stealing.

STUDY OBJECTIVE 4

Describe the applications of internal control principles to cash disbursements.

CONTROL OVER CASH DISBURSEMENTS

◆ Payments are made by check rather than by cash, except for petty cash transactions.

◆ Only specified individuals should be authorized to sign checks.

◆ Different departments or individuals should be assigned the duties of approving an item for payment and paying it.

CONTROL OVER CASH DISBURSEMENTS

◆ Prenumbered checks should be used and each check should be supported by an approved invoice or other document.

◆ Blank checks should be stored in a safe.

   1 Access should be restricted to authorized personnel.

   2 A check writer machine should be used to imprint the amount on the check in indelible ink.

CONTROL OVER CASH DISBURSEMENTS

◆ Each check should be compared with the approved invoice before it is issued.

◆ Following payment, the approved invoice should be stamped PAID.

VOUCHER SYSTEM

◆ The voucher system is often used to enhance the internal control over cash disbursements.

◆ It is an extensive network of approvals by authorized individuals acting independently to ensure that all disbursements by check are proper.

◆ A voucher is an authorization form prepared for each expenditure in a voucher system.

◆ Vouchers are recorded in a journal called the voucher register.

ELECTRONIC FUNDS TRANSFER SYSTEM

◆ Processing checks is expensive; therefore new methods are being developed to transfer funds among parties without the use of paper.

◆ Electronic Funds Transfer (EFT) System is a disbursement system that uses wire, telephone, telegraph, or computer to send cash from one location to another.

◆ Regular payments such as those for house, car, and utilities are frequently made by EFT.

STUDY OBJECTIVE 5

Explain the operation of a petty cash fund.

PETTY CASH FUND

◆ A petty cash fund is used to pay relatively small amounts

◆ Operation of the fund, often called an imprest system, involves:

   1 establishing the fund

   2 making payments from the fund

   3 replenishing the fund

◆ Accounting entries are required when:

   1 the fund is established

   2 the fund is replenished

   3 the amount of the fund is changed

ESTABLISHING THE FUND

◆ Two essential steps in establishing a petty cash fund are

1 appointing a petty cash custodian who will be responsible for the fund and

2 determining the size of the fund.

◆ Ordinarily, the amount is expected to cover anticipated disbursements for a 3- to 4-week period.

ESTABLISHING THE FUND

GENERAL JOURNAL

Date	Account Titles and Explanation	Debit	Credit
Mar. 1	Petty Cash	100	
	Cash		100
	(To establish a petty cash fund)		

When the fund is established, a check payable to the petty cash custodian is issued for the stipulated amount.

REPLENISHING THE FUND

◆ When the money in the petty cash fund reaches a minimum level, the fund is replenished.

◆ The request for reimbursement is initiated by the petty cash custodian.

◆ The petty cash custodian prepares a schedule of the payments that have been made and sends the schedule, with supporting documentation, to the treasurer's office.

REPLENISHING THE FUND

GENERAL JOURNAL

Date	Account Titles and Explanation	Debit	Credit
Mar. 15	Postage Expense	44	
	Freight-out	38	
	Miscellaneous Expense	5	
	Cash		87
	(To replenish petty cash fund)		

On March 15 the petty cash custodian requests a check for $87. The fund contains $13 cash and petty cash receipts for postage $44, freight-out $38, and miscellaneous expenses, $5.

REPLENISHING THE FUND

GENERAL JOURNAL

Date	Account Titles and Explanation	Debit	Credit
Mar. 15	Postage Expense	44	
	Freight-out	38	
	Miscellaneous Expense	5	
	Cash Over and Short	1	
	Cash		88
	(To replenish petty cash fund)		

On March 15 the petty cash custodian requests a check for $88. The fund contains $12 cash and petty cash receipts for postage $44, freight-out $38, and miscellaneous expenses, $5.

STUDY OBJECTIVE 6

Indicate the control features of a bank account.

USE OF A BANK

◆ The use of a bank minimizes the amount of currency that must be kept on hand and contributes significantly to good internal control over cash.

◆ A company can safeguard its cash by using a bank as a depository and clearing house for checks received and checks written.

WRITING CHECKS

◆ A check is a written order signed by the depositor directing the bank to pay a specified sum of money to a designated recipient.

◆ Three parties to a check are:

1 Maker (drawer) issues the check

2 Bank (payer) on which check is drawn

3 Payee to whom check is payable

BANK STATEMENTS

A bank statement shows:

1 checks paid and other debits charged against the account

2 deposits and other credits made to the account

3 account balance after each day's transactions

MEMORANDA

◆ Bank debit memoranda indicate charges against the depositor's account.

   Example: ATM service charges

◆ Bank credit memoranda indicate amounts that will increase the depositor's account.

   Example: interest income on account balance

STUDY OBJECTIVE 7

Prepare a bank reconciliation.

RECONCILING THE BANK ACCOUNT

◆ Reconciliation is necessary because the balance per bank and balance per books are seldom in agreement due to time lags and errors.

◆ A bank reconciliation should be prepared by an employee who has no other responsibilities pertaining to cash.

RECONCILING THE BANK ACCOUNT

◆ Steps in preparing a bank reconciliation:
  1 Determine deposits in transit
  2 Determine outstanding checks
  3 Note any errors discovered
  4 Trace bank memoranda to the records
◆ Each reconciling item used in determining the adjusted cash balance per books should be recorded by the depositor

---

ILLUSTRATION 7-14
BANK RECONCILIATION

LAIRD COMPANY
Bank Reconciliation
April 30, 1999

Cash balance per bank statement			$ 15,907.45
Add: Deposits in transit	The bank statement for the Laird Company shows a balance per bank of $15,907.45 on April 30, 1999.		2,201.40
			18,108.85
Less: Outstanding checks			
No. 453		$ 3,000.00	
No. 457		1,401.30	
No. 460		1,502.70	5,904.00
Adjusted cash balance per bank			$ 12,204.85
Cash balance per books			$ 11,589.45
Add: Collection of note receivable, $1,000 plus interest earned			
$50, less collection fee $15		$ 1,035.00	
Error in recording check No. 443		36.00	1,071.00
			12,660.45
Less: NSF check	On this date the balance of cash per books is $11,589.45.	425.60	
Bank service charge		30.00	455.60
Adjusted cash balance per books			$ 12,204.85

ENTRIES FROM BANK RECONCILIATION

GENERAL JOURNAL

Date	Account Titles and Explanation	Debit	Credit
Apr. 30	Cash	1,035.00	
	Miscellaneous Expense	15.00	
	Notes Receivable		1,000.00
	Interest Revenue		50.00
	(To record collection of notes receivable by bank)		

Collection of Note Receivable This entry involves four accounts. Interest of $50 has not been accrued and the collection fee is charged to Miscellaneous Expense.

ENTRIES FROM BANK RECONCILIATION

GENERAL JOURNAL

Date	Account Titles and Explanation	Debit	Credit
Apr. 30	Cash	36.00	
	Accounts Payable — Andrea Company		36.00
	(To correct error in recording check No. 443)		

Book Error An examination of the cash disbursements journal shows that check No. 443 was a payment on account to Andrea Company, a supplier. The check, with a correct amount of $1,226.00, was recorded at $1,262.00.

ENTRIES FROM BANK RECONCILIATION

GENERAL JOURNAL

Date	Account Titles and Explanation	Debit	Credit
Apr. 30	Accounts Receivable — J. R. Baron	425.60	
	Cash		425.60
	(To record NSF check)		

NSF Check An NSF check becomes an accounts receivable to the depositor.

ENTRIES FROM BANK RECONCILIATION

GENERAL JOURNAL

Date	Account Titles and Explanation	Debit	Credit
Apr. 30	Miscellaneous Expense	30.00	
	Cash		30.00
	(To record charge for printing company checks)		

Bank Service Charges Check printing charges (DM) and other bank service charges (SC) are debited to Miscellaneous Expense because they are usually nominal in amount.

STUDY OBJECTIVE 8

Explain the reporting of cash.

REPORTING CASH

◆ Cash reported on the Balance Sheet includes:

1 Cash on Hand

2 Cash in banks

3 Petty Cash

◆ Cash is listed first in the balance sheet under the title cash and cash equivalents because it is the most liquid asset.

CASH EQUIVALENTS

◆ Cash equivalents are highly liquid investments with maturities of 3 months or less when purchased that can be converted into a specific amount of cash.

◆ Examples include money market funds, bank certificates of deposit, and U.S. Treasury bills and notes.

CHAPTER 7
INTERNAL CONTROL AND CASH

WILEY
Publishers Since 1807

Accounting Principles, 5e
Weygandt, Kieso, & Kimmel

Prepared by
Marianne Bradford
The University of Mississippi
Gregory K. Lowry
Mercer University

John Wiley & Sons, Inc.

CHAPTER 8
ACCOUNTING FOR RECEIVABLES

After studying this chapter, you should be able to:

1 Identify the different types of receivables.
2 Explain how accounts receivable are recognized in the accounts.
3 Distinguish between the methods and bases used to value accounts receivable.
4 Describe the entries to record the disposition of accounts receivable.
5 Compute the maturity date of, and interest on, notes receivable.

CHAPTER 8
ACCOUNTING FOR RECEIVABLES

After studying this chapter, you should be able to:

6 Explain how notes receivable are recognized in the accounts.
7 Describe how notes receivable are valued.
8 Describe the entries to record the disposition of notes receivable.
9 Explain the statement presentation and analysis of receivables.

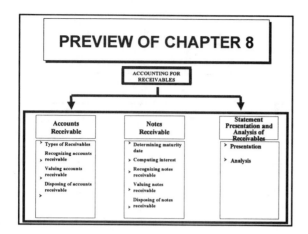

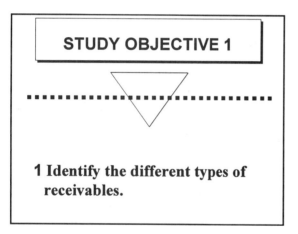

RECEIVABLES

● The term receivables refers to amounts due from individuals and other companies; they are claims expected to be collected in cash.

● Three major classes of receivables are:

1 Accounts Receivable - amounts owed by customers on account

2 Notes Receivable - claims for which formal instruments of credit are issued

3 Other Receivables - include nontrade receivables such as interest receivable and advances to employees

ACCOUNTS RECEIVABLE

The three primary accounting problems associated with accounts receivable are:

1 Recognizing accounts receivable.

2 Valuing accounts receivable.

3 Disposing of accounts receivable.

STUDY OBJECTIVE 2

2 Explain how accounts receivable are recognized in the accounts.

RECOGNIZING ACCOUNTS RECEIVABLE

Accounts Receivable – Polo Company	1,000	
Sales		1,000
(To record sales on account)		

When a business sells merchandise to a customer on credit, Accounts Receivable is debited and Sales is credited.

RECOGNIZING ACCOUNTS RECEIVABLE

Sales Returns and Allowances	100	
Accounts Receivable – Polo Company		100
(To record merchandise returned)		

When a business receives returned merchandise previously sold to a customer on credit, Sales Returns and Allowances is debited and Accounts Receivable is credited.

RECOGNIZING ACCOUNTS RECEIVABLE

Cash ($900-$18)	882	
Sales Discounts ($900 x .02)	18	
Accounts Receivable – Polo Company		900
(To record collection of AR)		

When a business collects cash from a customer for merchandise previously sold on credit during the discount period, Cash and Sales Discounts are debited and Accounts Receivable is credited.

STUDY OBJECTIVE 3

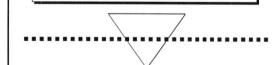

3 Distinguish between the methods and bases used to value accounts receivable

VALUING ACCOUNTS RECEIVABLE

- To ensure that receivables are not overstated on the balance sheet, they are stated at their cash realizable value.
- Cash (net) realizable value is the net amount expected to be received in cash and excludes amounts that the company estimates it will not be able to collect.
- Credit losses are debited to Bad Debts Expense and are considered a normal and necessary risk of doing business.
- Two methods of accounting for uncollectible accounts are:
  1 Allowance method
  2 Direct write-off method

THE ALLOWANCE METHOD

- The allowance method is required when bad debts are deemed to be material in amount.
- Uncollectible accounts are estimated and the expense for the uncollectible accounts is matched against sales in the same accounting period in which the sales occurred.

THE ALLOWANCE METHOD

GENERAL JOURNAL		
Dec. 31 Bad Debts Expense	12,000	
Allowance for Doubtful Accounts		12,000
(To record estimate of uncollectible accounts)		

Estimated uncollectibles are debited to Bad Debts Expense and credited to Allowance for Doubtful Accounts at the end of each period.

THE ALLOWANCE METHOD

GENERAL JOURNAL		
Mar. 1 Allowance for Doubtful Accounts	500	
Accounts Receivable — R. A. Ware		500
(Write-off of R. A. Ware account)		

Actual uncollectibles are debited to Allowance for Doubtful Accounts and credited to Accounts Receivable at the time the specific account is written off.

THE ALLOWANCE METHOD

GENERAL JOURNAL		
July 1 Accounts Receivable — R. A. Ware	500	
Allowance for Doubtful Accounts		500
(To reverse write-off of R. A. Ware account)		

When there is recovery of an account that has been written off:
1 reverse the entry made to write off the account and...

THE ALLOWANCE METHOD

GENERAL JOURNAL		
July 1 Cash	500	
Accounts Receivable — R. A. Ware		500
(To record collection from R. A. Ware)		

2 Record the collection in the usual manner.

BASES USED FOR THE ALLOWANCE METHOD

- Companies use either of two methods in the estimation of uncollectibles:

1 Percentage of sales

2 Percentage of receivables

- Both bases are GAAP; the choice is a management decision.

ILLUSTRATION 8-4
COMPARISON OF BASES OF ESTIMATING UNCOLLECTIBLES

Percentage of Sales	
Matching	
Sales ⟷	Bad Debts Expense

Empasis on Income Statement Relationships

Percentage of Receivables	
Cash Realizable Value	
Accounts Receivable ⟷	Allowance for Doubtful Accounts

Empasis on Balance Sheet Relationships

PERCENTAGE OF SALES BASIS

- In the percentage of sales basis, management establishes a percentage relationship between the amount of credit sales and expected losses from uncollectible accounts.
- Expected bad debt losses are determined by applying the percentage to the sales base of the current period.
- This basis better matches expenses with revenues.

PERCENTAGE OF SALES BASIS

GENERAL JOURNAL		
Dec. 31	Bad Debts Expense	8,000	
	Allowance for Doubtful Accounts		8,000
	(To record estimated bad debts for year)		

If net credit sales for the year are $800,000, the estimated bad debts expense is $8,000 (1% X $800,000).

PERCENTAGE OF RECEIVABLES BASIS

- Under the percentage of receivables basis, the balance in the allowance account is derived from an analysis of individual customer accounts often called aging the accounts receivable.
- The amount of the adjusting entry is the difference between the required balance and the existing balance in the allowance account.
- This basis produces the better estimate of cash realizable value of receivables.

PERCENTAGE OF RECEIVABLES BASIS

GENERAL JOURNAL		
Dec. 31	Bad Debts Expense	1,700	
	Allowance for Doubtful Accounts		1,700
	(To record estimated bad debts for year)		

If the trial balance shows Allowance for Doubtful Accounts with a credit balance of $528, an adjusting entry for $,1,700 ($2,228 - $528) is necessary.

DIRECT WRITE-OFF METHOD

- Under the direct write-off method, bad debt losses are not anticipated and no allowance account is used.
- No entries are made for bad debts until an account is determined to be uncollectible at which time the loss is charged to Bad Debts Expense.
- No attempt is made to match bad debts to sales revenues or to show cash realizable value of accounts receivable on the balance sheet.
- Consequently, unless bad debt losses are insignificant, this method is not acceptable for financial reporting purposes.

DIRECT WRITE-OFF METHOD

GENERAL JOURNAL		
Dec. 12 Bad Debts Expense	200	
Accounts Receivable — M. E. Doran (To record write-off of M. E. Doran account)		200

Warden Co. writes off M. E. Doran's $200 balance as uncollectible on December 12. When this method is used, Bad Debts Expense will show only actual losses from uncollectibles.

STUDY OBJECTIVE 4

4 Describe the entries to record the disposition of accounts receivable.

DISPOSING OF ACCOUNTS RECEIVABLE

- To accelerate the receipt of cash from receivables, owners frequently:
  1. sell to a factor such as a finance company or a bank and
  2. make credit card sales
- A factor buys receivables from businesses for a fee and collects the payments directly from customers.

SALE OF RECEIVABLES

GENERAL JOURNAL		
July 31 Cash	588,000	
Service Charge Expense (2% x $600,000)	12,000	
Accounts Receivable		600,000
(To record the sale of accounts receivable)		

Hendrendon Furniture factors $600,000 of receivables to Federal Factors, Inc. Federal Factors assesses a service charge of 2% of the amount of receivables sold.

CREDIT CARD SALES

- Credit cards are frequently used by retailers who wish to avoid the paperwork of issuing credit.
- Retailers can receive cash more quickly from the credit card issuer.
- A credit card sale occurs when a company accepts national credit cards, such as Visa, Mastercard, Discover, and American Express.

CREDIT CARD SALES

- Three parties involved when credit cards are used in making retail sales are:
  1 the credit card issuer,
  2 the retailer, and
  3 the customer.
- The retailer pays the credit card issuer a fee of 2-6% of the invoice price for its services.
- From an accounting standpoint, sales from Visa, Mastercard, and Discover are treated differently than sales from American Express.

_____

_____

_____

_____

_____

_____

_____

VISA, MASTERCARD, AND DISCOVER SALES

- Sales resulting from the use of VISA, MasterCard, and Discover are considered cash sales by the retailer.
- These cards are issued by banks.
- Upon receipt of credit card sales slips from a retailer, the bank immediately adds the amount to the seller's bank balance.

_____

_____

_____

_____

_____

_____

VISA, MASTERCARD, AND DISCOVER SALES

GENERAL JOURNAL		
July 31 Cash	970	
Service Charge Expense	30	
Sales		1,000
(To record VISA credit card sales)		

Anita Ferreri purchases a number of compact discs for her restaurant from Karen Kerr Music Co. for $1,000 using her VISA First Bank Card. The service fee that First Bank charges is 3%.

_____

_____

_____

_____

_____

_____

AMERICAN EXPRESS SALES

- Sales using American Express cards are reported as credit sales, not cash sales.

- Conversion into cash does not occur until American Express remits the net amount to the seller.

AMERICAN EXPRESS SALES

GENERAL JOURNAL		
July 31 Cash	285	
Service Charge Expense	15	
Sales		300
(To record VISA credit card sales)		

Four Seasons for her restaurant from Karen Kerr Music Co. for $1,000 using her VISA First Bank Card. The service fee that First Bank charges is 3%.

NOTES RECEIVABLE

- A promissory note is a written promise to pay a specified amount of money on demand or at a definite time.

- The party making the promise is the maker.

- The party to whom payment is made is called the payee.

NOTES RECEIVABLE

- When the life of the note is expressed in terms of months, the due date is found by counting the months from the date of issue
- Example: The maturity date of a 3-month note dated May 31 is August 31.

STUDY OBJECTIVE 5

5 Compute the maturity date of, and interest on, notes receivable.

DETERMINING THE MATURITY DATE

- When the life of the note is expressed in terms of days, it is necessary to count the days.
- In counting days, the date of issue is omitted but the due date is included.
- Example: The maturity date of a 60-day note dated July 17 is:

Term of note		60
July 31 - 17	14	
August	31	45
Maturity date, September		15

ILLUSTRATION 8-12
FORMULA FOR
COMPUTING INTEREST

The basic formula for computing interest on an interest-bearing note is:

| Face Value of Note | x | Annual Interest Rate | x | Time in Terms of One Year | = | Interest |

The interest rate specified on the note is an annual rate of interest.

ILLUSTRATION 8-13
COMPUTATION OF INTEREST

Terms of Note	Interest Computation					
	Face	X	Rate	X	Time	=	Interest
$ 730, 18%, 120 days	$ 730	X	18%	X	120/360	=	$ 43.80
$1,000, 15%, 6 months	$1,000	X	15%	X	6/12	=	$ 75.00
$2,000, 12%, 1 year	$2,000	X	12%	X	1/1	=	$240.00

Helpful hint: The interest rate specified is the annual rate.

STUDY OBJECTIVE 6

6 Explain how notes receivable are recognized in the accounts.

RECOGNIZING NOTES RECEIVABLE

GENERAL JOURNAL		
May 1	Notes Receivable	1,000	
	Accounts Receivable — Brent Company		1,000
	(To record acceptance of Brent		
	Company note)		

Wilma Company receives a $1,000, 2-month, 12% promissory note from Brent Company to settle an open account.

STUDY OBJECTIVE 7

▼

7 Describe how notes receivable are valued.

VALUING NOTES RECEIVABLE

- Like accounts receivable, short-term notes receivable are reported at their cash (net) realizable value.
- The notes receivable allowance account is Allowance for Doubtful Accounts.

STUDY OBJECTIVE 8

8 Describe the entries to record the disposition of notes receivable.

HONOR OF NOTES RECEIVABLE

Oct 1.	Cash	10,300	
	Notes Receivable		10,000
	Interest Revenue		300
	(To record collection of Higley Inc. note)		

● A note is honored when it is paid in full at its maturity date.

● For each interest-bearing note, the amount due at maturity is the face value of the note plus interest for the length of time specified on the note.

● Betty Co. lends Wayne Higley Inc. $10,000 on June 1, accepting a 4-month, 9% interest-bearing note.

● Betty collects the maturity value of the note from Higley on October 1.

HONOR OF NOTES RECEIVABLE

Sept 30.	Interest Receivable	300	
	Interest Revenue		300
	(To accrue 4 months' interest)		

If Betty Co. prepares prepares financial statements as of September 30, interest for 4 months, or $300, would be accrued.

HONOR OF NOTES RECEIVABLE

Oct. 1	Cash	10,300	
	Notes Receivable		10,000
	Interest Receivable		300
	(To record collection of note at maturity)		

When interest has been accrued, it is necessary to credit Interest Receivable at maturity.

DISHONOR OF NOTES RECEIVABLE

GENERAL JOURNAL

Oct. 1	Accounts Receivable	10,300	
	Notes Receivable		10,000
	Interest Revenue		300
	(To record the dishonor of the note)		

- A dishonored note is a note that is not paid in full at maturity.
- A dishonored note receivable is no longer negotiable.
- Since the payee still has a claim against the maker of the note, the balance in Notes Receivable is usually transferred to Accounts Receivable.

STUDY OBJECTIVE 9

9 Explain the statement presentation and analysis of receivables.

ILLUSTRATION 8-14
BALANCE SHEET PRESENTATION
OF RECEIVABLES

- In the balance sheet, short-term receivables are reported within the current assets section below temporary investments.
- Report both the *gross amount of receivables* and the *allowance for doubtful accounts*.
- The current asset presenation of receivables for Kellogg Co. at December 31, 1997 is shown below:

Kellogg Co.	
Accounts receivable (in millions)	$ 595.0
Less: Allowance for doubtful accounts	7.5
Net receivables	$ 587.5

ILLUSTRATION 8-15
ACCOUNTS RECEIVABLE TURNOVER
RATIO AND COMPUTATION

- Financial ratios are computed to evaluate the liquidity of a company's accounts receivable.
- The ratio used to assess the liquidity of the receivables is the receivables turnover ratio.
- If Kellogg had net credit sales of $6,830.1 million for the year and beginning net accounts receivable balance of $592.3 million, its turnover ratio is computed as follows:

Net Credit Sales	/	Average Net Receivables	=	Accounts Receivable Turnover

$6,830.1   / ($592.3 + $587.5)/2 =   11.6 times

ILLUSTRATION 8-16
AVERAGE COLLECTION PERIOD FOR
RECEIVABLES FORMULA AND
COMPUTATION

- The average collection period in days is a variant of the turnover ratio that makes liquidity even more evident.
- This is done by dividing the turnover ratio into 365 days. The *general rule* is that the collection period should not exceed the credit term period.
- Kellogg's turnover ratio is computed as:

Days in Year	/	Accounts Receivable Turnover	=	Average Collection Period in Days

365 days   /   11.6 times   =   31.5 days

Accounting Principles, 5e
Weygandt, Kieso, & Kimmel

Prepared by
Marianne Bradford
The University of Tennessee
Gregory K. Lowry
Mercer University

John Wiley & Sons, Inc.

CHAPTER 9
INVENTORIES

After studying this chapter, you should be able to:

1 Describe the steps in determining inventory quantities.
2 Prepare the entries for purchases and sales of inventory under a periodic inventory system.
3 Determine cost of goods sold under a periodic inventory system.
4 Identify the unique features of the income statement for a merchandising company using a periodic inventory system.
5 Explain the basis of accounting for inventories and describe the inventory cost flow methods.

CHAPTER 9
INVENTORIES

After studying this chapter, you should be able to:

6 Explain the financial statement and tax effects of each of the inventory cost flow methods.
7 Explain the lower of cost or market basis of accounting for inventories.
8 Indicate the effects of inventory errors on the financial statements.
9 Compute and interpret the inventory turnover ratio.

PREVIEW OF CHAPTER 9

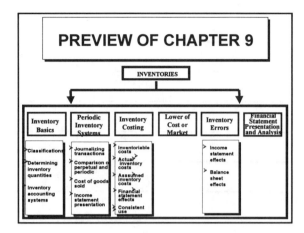

INVENTORIES

Inventory Basics	Periodic Inventory Systems	Inventory Costing	Lower of Cost or Market	Inventory Errors	Financial Statement Presentation and Analysis
Classifications	Journalizing transactions	Inventoriable costs		Income statement effects	
Determining inventory quantities	Comparison of perpetual and periodic	Actual inventory costs		Balance sheet effects	
Inventory accounting systems	Cost of goods sold	Assumed inventory costs			
	Income statement presentation	Financial statement effects			
		Consistent use			

INVENTORY BASICS

- In the balance sheet of merchandising and manufacturing companies, inventory is frequently the most significant current asset.
- In the income statement, inventory is vital in determining the results of operations for a particular period.
- Gross profit (net sales - cost of goods sold) is closely watched by management, owners, and other interested parties.

MERCHANDISE INVENTORY CHARACTERISTICS

Merchandise inventory has two common characteristics:

1 it is owned by the company and

2 it is in a form ready for sale to customers in the ordinary course of business

CLASSIFYING INVENTORY IN A MANUFACTURING ENVIRONMENT

- Unlike merchandise inventory, manufacturing inventory may not yet be ready for sale.
- As a result, inventory is usually classified into three categories:

  1 Finished goods, inventory which is completed and ready for sale.

  2 Work in process, inventory in various stages of production but not yet completed.

  3 Raw materials, components on hand waiting to be used in production.

STUDY OBJECTIVE 1

1 Describe the steps in determining inventory quantities.

DETERMINING INVENTORY QUANTITIES

- In order to prepare financial statements, it is necessary to determine the number of units of inventory owned by the company at the statement date, and to value them.
- The determination of inventory quantities involves

  1 taking a physical inventory of goods on hand

  2 determining the ownership of goods.
- Taking a physical inventory involves counting, weighing or measuring each kind of inventory on hand.

TAKING A PHYSICAL INVENTORY

A company, in order to minimize errors in taking the inventory, should adhere to internal control principles by adopting the following procedures:

1 Employees who do not have custodial responsibility for the inventory should do the counting. (Segregation of duties)

2 Each counter should establish the authenticity of each inventory item. (Establishment of responsibility)

TAKING A PHYSICAL INVENTORY

3 Another employee should make a second count. (Independent internal verification)

4 All inventory tags should be prenumbered and accounted for. (Documentation procedures)

5 At the end of the count, a designated supervisor should ascertain that all inventory items are tagged and that no items have more than one tag. (Independent internal verification)

DETERMINING OWNERSHIP OF GOODS IN TRANSIT

- Goods in transit should be included in the inventory of the party that has legal title to the goods.
- For FOB (Free on Board) shipping point, ownership of the goods passes to the buyer when the public carrier accepts the goods from the seller.
- For FOB destination point, legal title to the goods remains with the seller until the goods reach the buyer.

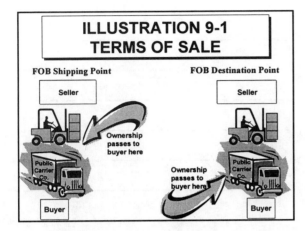

ILLUSTRATION 9-1
TERMS OF SALE

FOB Shipping Point

FOB Destination Point

DETERMINING OWNERSHIP OF GOODS IN TRANSIT

- Under a consignment arrangement, the holder of the goods (called the consignee) does not own the goods.
- Ownership remains with the shipper of the goods (consignor) until the goods are actually sold to a customer.
- Consigned goods should be included in the consignor's inventory not the consignee's inventory.

Owned by a consignor; do not count in our consignee inventory

Consignee Company

INVENTORY ACCOUNTING SYSTEMS

Merchandising entities may use either of the following inventory systems:

1 Perpetual

Detailed records of the cost of each item are maintained, and the cost of each item sold is determined from records when the sale occurs.

2 Periodic

Cost of goods sold is determined only at the end of an accounting period not after each sale.

STUDY OBJECTIVE 2

2 Prepare the entries for purchases and sales of inventory under a periodic inventory system.

PERIODIC INVENTORY SYSTEMS

- Revenues from the sale of merchandise are recorded when sales are made in the same way as in a perpetual system.
- No attempt is made on the date of sale to record the cost of merchandise sold.
- Physical inventories are taken at end of period to determine:
  - the cost of merchandise on hand
  - the cost of the goods sold during the period

RECORDING MERCHANDISE TRANSACTIONS UNDER A PERIODIC INVENTORY SYSTEM

- When merchandise is purchased for resale to customers, the temporary account, Purchases, is debited for the cost of goods.
- Like sales, purchases may be made for cash or on account (credit).
- The purchase is normally recorded by the purchaser when the goods are received from the seller.
- Each credit purchase should be supported by a purchase invoice.

RECORDING PURCHASES OF MERCHANDISE

GENERAL JOURNAL			
May 4	Purchases	3,800	
	Accounts Payable		3,800
	(To record goods purchased on account, terms 2/10, n/30)		

To illustrate the recording of merchandise transactions under a periodic system, we will use the purchase/sale transactions between Highpoint Electronic and Chelsea Video. For purchases on account, Chelsea Video records Purchases is debited and Accounts Payable is credited for merchandise ordered from Highpoint Electronic.

PURCHASE RETURNS AND ALLOWANCES

- A sales return and allowance on the seller's books is recorded as a purchase return and allowance on the books of the purchaser.
- Purchase Returns and Allowances is a contra account to Purchases and has a normal credit balance.
- The purchaser initiates the request for a reduction of the balance due through the issuance of a debit memorandum.
- The debit memorandum is a document issued by a buyer to inform a seller that the seller's account has been debited because of unsatisfactory merchandise.

RECORDING PURCHASE RETURNS AND ALLOWANCES

GENERAL JOURNAL			
May 8	Accounts Payable	300	
	Purchase Returns and Allowances		300
	(To record allowance for damaged goods)		

For purchases returns and allowances, Accounts Payable is debited and Purchase Returns and Allowances is credited. Because $300 of merchandise received from Highpoint Electronic is inoperable, Chelsea Video returns the goods and issues a debit memo.

FREE ON BOARD

- The sales agreement should indicate whether the seller or the buyer is to pay the cost of transporting the goods to the buyer's place of business.
- FOB Shipping Point
  1 Goods placed free on board the carrier by seller
  2 Buyer pays freight costs
- FOB Destination
  1 Goods placed free on board at buyer's business
  2 Seller pays freight costs

ACCOUNTING FOR FREIGHT COSTS

- Freight-in is debited if buyer pays freight
- Freight-out (or Delivery Expense) is debited if seller pays freight.

ACCOUNTING FOR FREIGHT COSTS

GENERAL JOURNAL			
May 6	Freight-in	150	
	Cash		150
	(To record payment of freight, terms FOB shipping point)		

When the purchaser directly incurs the freight costs, the account Freight-in (or Transportation-in) is debited and Cash is credited. In this example, ChelseaVideo pays Acme Freight Company $150 for freight charges on its purchase from Highpoint Electronic.

PURCHASE DISCOUNTS

- Credit terms may permit the buyer to claim a cash discount for the prompt payment of a balance due.
- The buyer calls this discount a purchase discount.
- Like a sales discount, a purchase discount is based on the invoice cost less returns and allowances, if any.

PURCHASE DISCOUNTS

GENERAL JOURNAL		
May 14 Accounts Payable	3,500	
Purchase Discounts		70
Cash		3,430
(To record payment within discount period)		

If payment is made within the discount period, Accounts Payable is debited, Purchase Discounts is credited for the discount taken, and Cash is credited. On May 14 Chelsea Video pays the balance due on account to Highpoint Electronic taking the 2% cash discount allowed by Highpoint for payment within 10 days.

SALES TRANSACTIONS

- Revenues are reported when earned in accordance with the revenue recognition principle, and in a merchandising company, revenues are earned when the goods are transferred from seller to buyer.
- All sales should be supported by a document such as a cash register tape or sales invoice.

RECORDING SALES OF MERCHANDISE

GENERAL JOURNAL			
May 4	Accounts Receivable	3,800	
	Sales		3,800
	(To credit sales per invoice #731)		

For credit sales, Accounts Receivable is debited and Sales is credited. In this illustration, the sale of $3,800 of merchandise to Chelsea Video on May 4 is recorded by the seller, Highpoint Electronic.

SALES RETURNS AND ALLOWANCES

- Sales Returns result when customers are dissatisfied with merchandise and are allowed to return the goods to the seller for credit or a refund.
- Sales Allowances result when customers are dissatisfied, and the seller allows a deduction from the selling price.

SALES RETURNS AND ALLOWANCES

- To grant the return or allowance, the seller prepares a credit memorandum to inform the customer that a credit has been made to the customer's account receivable.
- Sales Returns and Allowances is a contra revenue account to the Sales account.
- The normal balance of Sales Returns and Allowances is a debit.

RECORDING SALES RETURNS AND ALLOWANCES

GENERAL JOURNAL			
May 8	Sales Returns and Allowances	300	
	Accounts Receivable		300
	(To record allowance for damaged goods per credit memorandum CM126)		

The seller's entry to record a credit memorandum involves a debit to the Sales Returns and Allowances account and a credit to Accounts Receivable. Based on the debit memo received from Chelsea Video on May 8 for returned goods, Highpoint Electronic records the $300 sales returns above.

SALES DISCOUNTS

- A sales discount is the offer of a cash discount to a customer for the prompt payment of a balance due.
- Example: If a credit sale has the terms 3/10, n/30, a 3% discount is allowed if payment is made within 10 days. After 10 days there is no discount, and the balance is due in 30 days.
- Sales Discounts is a *contra revenue account* with a normal debit balance.

CREDIT TERMS

- Credit terms specify the amount and time period for the cash discount.
- They also indicate the length of time in which the purchaser is expected to pay the full invoice price.

TERMS	EXPLANATION
2/10, n/30	A 2% discount may be taken if payment is made within 10 days of the invoice data.
1/10 EOM	A 1% discount is available if payment is made by the 10th of the next month.

RECORDING SALES DISCOUNTS

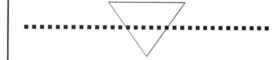

GENERAL JOURNAL

May 15	Cash	3,430	
	Sales Discounts	70	
	Accounts Receivable		3,500
	(To record collection within		
	2/10, n/30 discount period)		

When cash discounts are taken by customers, the seller debits Sales Discounts. On May 15, Highpoint Electronic receives payment of $3,430 on account from Chelsea Video. Highpoint honrs the 2% discount and records the payment of Chelsea's accounts receivable.

STUDY OBJECTIVE 3

3 Determine cost of goods sold under a periodic inventory system.

COST OF GOODS SOLD

To determine the cost of goods sold under a *periodic inventory system*, it is necessary to:

1 record purchases of merchandise,

2 determine the cost of goods purchased, and

3 determine the cost of goods on hand at the beginning and end of the accounting period.

ILLUSTRATION 9-3
NORMAL BALANCES; COST OF
GOODS PURCHASED ACCOUNTS

Account	Normal Balance
Purchases	Debit
Purchase Returns and Allowances	Credit
Purchase Discounts	Credit
Freight-in	Debit

ALLOCATING INVENTORIABLE COSTS

- Inventoriable costs are allocated between ending inventory and cost of goods sold.
- Under a periodic inventory system, the allocation is made at the end of the accounting period.

1 The costs assignable to the ending inventory are determined.

2 The cost of the ending inventory is subtracted from the cost of goods available for sale to determine the cost of goods sold.

3 Cost of goods sold is then deducted from sales revenues in accordance with the matching principle.

DETERMINING COST OF GOODS PURCHASED

To determine Cost of Goods Purchased:

1 Subtract contra purchase accounts from purchases to get net purchases

2 Add freight-in to net purchases

ILLUSTRATION 9-4
COMPUTATION OF NET PURCHASES
AND COST OF GOODS PURCHASED

Cost of Goods Purchased is determined as follows:

Purchases		$ 325,000
Less: Purchases returns and allowances	$10,400	
Purchase discounts	6,800	17,200
Net purchases		307,800
Add: Freight-in		12,200
Cost of goods purchased		$ 320,000

DETERMINING COST OF GOODS ON HAND

Under the periodic method, cost of inventory on hand is determined from a physical inventory requiring:

1 Counting the units on hand for each inventory item.

2 Applying unit costs to the total units on hand for each inventory item.

3 Aggregating the cost of each item of inventory to determine total cost of goods on hand.

ILLUSTRATION 9-5
COMPUTATION OF COST OF GOODS AVAILABLE
FOR SALE AND COST OF GOODS SOLD

Cost of Goods Sold is determined as follows:

Beginning inventory	$ 36,000
Add: Cost of goods purchased	320,000
Cost of goods available for sale	356,000
Less: Ending inventory	40,000
Cost of goods sold	$ 316,000

STUDY OBJECTIVE 4

4   Identify the unique features of the income statement for a merchandising company using a periodic inventory system.

COMPUTATION OF GROSS PROFIT

Gross profit is determined as follows:

Net sales	$ 460,000
Cost of goods sold	316,000
Gross profit	$ 144,000

OPERATING EXPENSES IN COMPUTING NET INCOME

Net income is determined as follows:

Gross profit	$ 144,000
Operating expenses	114,000
Net income	$ 30,000

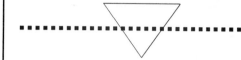

STUDY OBJECTIVE 5

5 Explain the basis of accounting for inventories and describe the inventory cost flow methods.

ILLUSTRATION 9-7
ALLOCATION (MATCHING)
OF POOL OF COSTS

Pool of Costs	
Cost of Goods Available for Sale	
Beginning inventory	$ 20,000
Cost of goods purchased	100,000
Cost of goods available for sale	$ 120,000

Step 1			Step 2	
Ending Inventory			**Cost of Goods Sold**	
Units	Unit Cost	Total Cost	Cost of goods available for sale	$120,000
			Less: Ending inventory	15,000
5,000	$ 3.00	$15,000	Cost of goods sold	$105,000

USING ACTUAL PHYSICAL FLOW COSTING

- Costing of the inventory is complicated because the units on hand for a specific item of inventory may have been purchased at different prices.
- The specific identification method tracks the actual physical flow of the goods.
- Each item of inventory is marked, tagged, or coded with its specific unit cost.
- Items still in inventory at the end of the year are specifically costed to arrive at the total cost of the ending inventory.

USING ASSUMED COST FLOW METHODS

- Other cost flow methods are allowed since specific identification is often impractical.
- These methods assume flows of costs that may be unrelated to the physical flow of goods.
- For this reason we call them assumed cost flow methods or cost flow assumptions. They are:

1 First-in, first-out (FIFO).

2 Last-in, first-out (LIFO).

3 Average cost.

FIFO

- The FIFO method assumes that the earliest goods purchased are the first to be sold.
- FIFO often reflects the actual physical flow of merchandise since it is normally sound business practice to sell the oldest units first.
- Therefore, under FIFO, the costs of the earliest goods purchased are the first to be recognized as cost of goods sold.

ILLUSTRATION 9-10 ALLOCATION OF COSTS - FIFO METHOD

Pool of Costs

Cost of Goods Available for Sale

Date	Explanation	Units	Unit Cost	Total Cost
01/01	Beginning Inventory	100	$10	$ 1,000
04/15	Purchase	200	11	2,200
08/24	Purchase	300	12	3,600
11/27	Purchase	400	13	5,200
	Total	1,000		$ 12,000

Step 1			Step 2	
Ending Inventory			**Cost of Goods Sold**	

Date	Units	Unit Cost	Total Cost		
11/27	400	$ 13	$ 5,200	Cost of goods available for sale	$ 12,000
08/24	50	12	600	Less: Ending inventory	5,800
	450		$ 5,800	Cost of goods sold	$ 6,200

ILLUSTRATION 9-12
PROOF OF COST OF GOODS SOLD

The accuracy of the cost of goods sold can be verified by recognizing that the first units acquired are the first units sold.

Date	Units		Unit Cost		Total Cost
01/01	100	X	$ 10	=	$ 1,000
04/15	200	X	11	=	2,200
08/24	250	X	12	=	3,000
Total	550				$ 6,200

LIFO

- The LIFO method assumes that the latest goods purchased are the first to be sold.
- LIFO seldom coincides with the actual physical flow of inventory.
- Under LIFO, the costs of the latest goods purchased are the first to be recognized as cost of goods sold.

ILLUSTRATION 9-13
ALLOCATION OF COSTS
- LIFO METHOD

Pool of Costs

Cost of Goods Available for Sale

Date	Explanation	Units	Unit Cost	Total Cost
01/01	Beginning Inventory	100	$10	$ 1,000
04/15	Purchase	200	11	2,200
08/24	Purchase	300	12	3,600
11/27	Purchase	400	13	5,200
	Total	1,000		$ 12,000

Step 1

Ending Inventory

Date	Units	Unit Cost	Total Cost
01/01	100	$ 10	$ 1,000
04/15	200	11	2,200
08/24	150	12	1,800
	450		$ 5,000

Step 2

Cost of Goods Sold

Cost of goods available for sale	$ 12,000
Less: Ending inventory	5,000
Cost of goods sold	$ 7,000

ILLUSTRATION 9-15
PROOF OF COST OF GOODS SOLD

The cost of the last goods in are the first to be assigned to cost of goods sold. Under a periodic inventory system, all goods purchased during the period are assumed to be available for the first sale, regardless of the date of purchase.

Date	Units		Unit Cost		Total Cost
11/27	400	X	$ 13	=	$ 5,200
08/24	150	X	12	=	1,800
Total	550				$ 7,000

AVERAGE COST

- The average cost method assumes that the goods available for sale are homogeneous.
- The allocation of the cost of goods available for sale is made on the basis of the weighted average unit cost incurred.
- The weighted average unit cost is then applied to the units on hand to determine the cost of the ending inventory.

ILLUSTRATION 9-17
ALLOCATION OF COSTS
- AVERAGE COST METHOD

	Pool of Costs			
	Cost of Goods Available for Sale			
Date	Explanation	Units	Unit Cost	Total Cost
01/01	Beginning inventory	100	$10	$ 1,000
04/15	Purchase	200	11	2,200
08/24	Purchase	300	12	3,600
11/27	Purchase	400	13	5,200
	Total	1,000		$ 12,000

Step 1			Step 2	
Ending Inventory			Cost of Goods Sold	
$ 12,000 ÷	1,000 =	$12.00		
Units	Unit Cost	Total Cost	Cost of goods available for sale	$ 12,000
			Less: Ending inventory	5,400
450 x	$ 12.00 =	$ 5,400	Cost of goods sold	$ 6,600

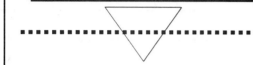

STUDY OBJECTIVE 6

6 Explain the financial statement and tax effects of each of the inventory cost flow methods.

ILLUSTRATION 9-19
USE OF COST FLOW METHODS
IN MAJOR U.S. COMPANIES

The reasons why companies adopt different inventory cost flow methods usually involve one of the following factors: 1 income statement effects, 2 balance sheet effects, or 3 tax effects.

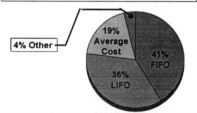

4% Other

19% Average Cost

41% FIFO

36% LIFO

ILLUSTRATION 9-21
INCOME STATEMENT EFFECTS
COMPARED

Kralik Company buys 200 XR492s at $20 per unit on January 10 and 200 more on December 31 at $24 each. During the year, 200 units are sold at $30 each. Under LIFO, the company recovers the current replacement cost ($4,800) of the units sold. Under FIFO, however, the company recovers only the January 10 cost ($4,000). To replace the units sold, it must invest $800 (200 x $4) of the gross profit. Thus, $800 of the gross profit is said to be phantom or illusory profits. As a result, reported net income is overstated in real terms.

	FIFO		Average Cost		LIFO	
Sales (200 x $30)	$ 6,000		$ 6,000		$ 6,000	
Cost of goods sold	4,000	(200 x $20)	4,400	(200 x $22)	4,800	(200 x $24)
Gross profit	$ 2,000		$ 1,600		$ 1,200	

USING INVENTORY COST FLOW METHODS CONSISTENTLY

- A company needs to use its chosen cost flow method consistently from one accounting period to another.
- Such consistent application enhances the comparability of financial statements over successive time periods.
- When a company adopts a different cost flow method, the change and its effects on net income should be disclosed in the financial statements.

STUDY OBJECTIVE 7

7 Explain the lower of cost or market basis of accounting for inventories.

VALUING INVENTORY AT THE LOWER OF COST OR MARKET

- When the value of inventory is lower than the cost, the inventory is written down to its market value.
- This is known as the lower of cost or market (LCM) method.
- Under the LCM basis, market is defined as current replacement cost, not selling price.

ILLUSTRATION 9-23
ALTERNATIVE LOWER OF COST OR MARKET

	Cost	Market	Lower of Cost or Market by: Individual Items	Major Categories	Total Inventory
Television sets					
Consoles	$ 60,000	$ 55,000	$ 55,000		
Portables	45,000	52,000	45,000		
Total	105,000	107,000		$ 105,000	
Video equipment					
Recorders	48,000	45,000	45,000		
Movies	15,000	14,000	14,000		
Total	63,000	59,000		59,000	
Total inventory	$ 168,000	$ 166,000	$ 159,000	$ 164,000	$ 166,000

STUDY OBJECTIVE 8

∙∙∙∙∙∙∙∙∙∙∙∙∙∙∙∙∙∙∙∙∙∙∙∙∙∙∙∙∙∙

▽

8 Indicate the effects of inventory errors on the financial statements.

INVENTORY ERRORS - INCOME STATEMENT EFFECTS

- Both beginning and ending inventories appear on the income statement.
- The ending inventory of one period automatically becomes the beginning inventory of the next period.
- Inventory errors affect the determination of cost of goods sold and net income.

ILLUSTRATION 9-24
FORMULA FOR
COST OF GOODS SOLD

| Beginning Inventory | + | Cost of Goods Purchased | − | Ending Inventory | = | Cost of Goods Sold |

The effects on cost of goods sold can be determined by entering the incorrect data in the above formula and then substituting the correct data.

ILLUSTRATION 9-25
EFFECTS OF INVENTORY ERRORS ON
CURRENT YEAR'S INCOME STATEMENT

Inventory Error	Cost of Goods Sold	Net Income
Understate beginning inventory	Understated	Overstated
Overstate beginning inventory	Overstated	Understated
Understate ending inventory	Overstated	Understated
Overstate ending inventory	Understated	Overstated

An error in ending inventory of the current period will have a reverse effect on net income of the next accounting period.

ENDING INVENTORY ERROR -
BALANCE SHEET EFFECTS

The effect of ending inventory errors on the balance sheet can be determined by using the basic accounting equation:

Assets = Liabilities + Owner's Equity

_____
_____
_____
_____
_____
_____
_____

_____
_____
_____
_____
_____
_____

_____
_____
_____
_____
_____
_____

ILLUSTRATION 9-27
ENDING INVENTORY ERROR - BALANCE SHEET EFFECTS

Errors in the ending inventory have the following effects on these components:

Ending Inventory Error	Assets	Liabilities	Owner's Equity
Overstated	Overstated	None	Overstated
Understated	Understated	None	Understated

ILLUSTRATION 9-28
INVENTORY DISCLOSURES

- Inventory is classified as a current asset after receivables in the balance sheet.
- Cost of goods sold is subtracted from sales in the income statement.
- There should be disclosure either in the balance sheet or in accompanying notes of:
  1 major inventory classifications
  2 basis of accounting (cost or lower of cost or market)
  3 costing method (FIFO, LIFO, or average cost)

KELLOGG COMPANY

Note 1. Accounting Policies
Inventories
Inventories are valued at the lower of cost (principally average) or market.

STUDY OBJECTIVE 9

9 Compute and interpret the inventory turnover ratio.

ILLUSTRATION 9-29
INVENTORY TURNOVER
FORMULA AND COMPUTATION

The inventory turnover ratio measures the number of times, on average, the inventory is sold during the period – which measures the liquidity of the inventory. It is calculated by dividing cost of goods sold by average inventory during the year. Assume that Kellogg Company has a beginning inventory of $424,900,000, ending inventory of $434,300,000 and cost of goods sold for 1997 of $3,270,100,000; its inventory turnover formula and computation is shown below:

$$\text{INVENTORY TURNOVER} = \frac{\text{COST OF GOODS SOLD}}{\text{AVERAGE INVENTORY}}$$

$$7.6 \text{ times} = \frac{\$3,270,100,000}{(\$424,900,000 + \$434,300,000)/2}$$

STUDY OBJECTIVE 10

10 Describe the two methods of estimating inventories

APPENDIX 9A
ESTIMATING INVENTORIES

- Two circumstances explain the reasons for estimating rather than counting inventories:
  1 Management may want monthly or quarterly financial statements, but a physical inventory is taken only annually.

  2 A casualty such as a fire or flood may make it impossible to take a physical inventory.
- There are two widely used methods of estimating inventories:
  1 the gross profit method and
  2 the retail inventory method.

GROSS PROFIT METHOD

- The gross profit method estimates the cost of ending inventory by applying a gross profit rate to net sales.
- It is used in preparing monthly financial statements when physical inventories are not taken.
- It should NOT be used in preparing the company's financial statements at year-end.
- The gross profit rate is assumed to remain constant from one year to the next.

ILLUSTRATION 9A-1
GROSS PROFIT METHOD FORMULAS

Step 1 Net sales less estimated gross profit equals estimated cost of goods sold.

Net Sales	—	Estimated Gross Profit	=	Estimated Cost of Goods Sold
Cost of Goods Available for Sale	—	Estimated Cost of Goods Sold	=	Estimated Cost of Ending Inventory

Step 2 Cost of goods available for sale less estimated cost of goods sold (from Step 1) equals the estimated cost of ending inventory.

RETAIL INVENTORY METHOD

- When a store has many different types of merchandise at low unit costs, the retail inventory method is often used.
- To use this method, a company must maintain records that show both the cost and retail value of the goods available for sale.
- The major disadvantage of this method is that it is an averaging technique.

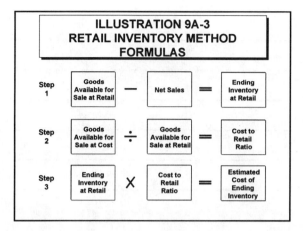

**ILLUSTRATION 9A-3
RETAIL INVENTORY METHOD FORMULAS**

STUDY OBJECTIVE 11

11 Apply the inventory cost flow methods to perpetual inventory records.

**APPENDIX 9B
INVENTORY COST FLOW METHODS IN PERPETUAL INVENTORY SYSTEMS**

To illustrate the application of the 3 assumed cost flow methods (FIFO, Average Cost, and LIFO), the data shown below for Bow Valley Electronics' product Z202 Astro Condenser is used.

Bow Valley Electronics
Z202 Astro Condensers

Date	Explanation	Units	Unit Cost	Total Cost
01/01	Beginning inventory	100	$10	$ 1,000
04/15	Purchase	200	11	2,200
08/24	Purchase	300	12	3,600
11/27	Purchase	400	13	5,200
	Total			$ 12,000

ILLUSTRATION 9B-2
PERPETUAL SYSTEM - FIFO

Under FIFO, the cost of the earliest goods on hand prior to each sale is charged to cost of goods sold. Therefore, the cost of goods sold on September 10 consists of the units on hand January 1 and the units purchased April 15 and August 24.

Date	Purchases	Sales	Balance	
January 1			(100 @ $10)	$1,00
April 15	(200 @ $11) $2,200		(100 @ $10) (200 @ $11)	$3,20
August 24	(300 @ $12) $3,600		(100 @ $10) (200 @ $11) (300 @ $12)	$6,80
September 10		(100 @ $10) (200 @ $11) $6,200 (250 @ $12)	(50 @ $12)	$600
November 27	(400 @ $13) $5,200		(50 @ $12) (400 @ $13)	$5,80

ILLUSTRATION 9B-3
PERPETUAL SYSTEM - LIFO

Under the LIFO method using a perpetual system, the cost of the most recent purchase prior to sale is allocated to the units sold. Therefore, the cost of the goods sold on September 10 consists entirely of goods from the August 24 and April 15 purchases and 50 of the units in beginning inventory.

Date	Purchases	Sales	Balance	
January 1			(100 @ $10)	$1,00
April 15	(200 @ $11) $2,200		(100 @ $10) (200 @ $11)	$3,20
August 24	(300 @ $12) $3,600		(100 @ $10) (200 @ $11) (300 @ $12)	$6,80
September 10		(300 @ $20) (200 @ $11) $6,300 (50 @ $10)	(50 @ $10)	$500
November 27	(400 @ $13) $5,200		(50 @ $10) (400 @ $13)	$5,70

PERPETUAL SYSTEM - AVERAGE COST

The average cost method in a perpetual inventory system is called the moving average method. Under this method a new average is calculated after each purchase. The average cost is calculated by dividing the cost of goods available for sale by the units on hand. The average cost is then applied to

1 the units sold, to determine the cost of goods sold, and

2 the remaining units on hand, to determine the amount of the ending inventory.

ILLUSTRATION 9B-4
PERPETUAL SYSTEM -
AVERAGE COST METHOD

As indicated below, a new average is computed each time a purchase is made. On April 15, after 200 units are purchased for $2,200, a total of 300 units costing $3,200 ($1,000 + $2,200) are on hand. The average cost is $10.667 ($3,200/300).

Date	Purchases	Sales	Balance
January 1			(100 @ $10) $1,000
April 15	(200 @ $11) $2,200		(300 @ 10.667) $3,200
August 24	(300 @ $12) $3,600		(600 @ 11.333) $6,800
September 10		(550 @ 11.333) $6,233	(50 @ $11.333) $567
November 27	(400 @ $13) $5,200		(450 @ 12.816) $5,767

CHAPTER 9
INVENTORIES

Chapter 10
Plant Assets, Natural Resources, and Intangible Assets

Accounting Principles, 5e
Weygandt, Kieso, & Kimmel

Prepared by
Marianne Bradford
The University of Tennessee
Gregory K. Lowry
Mercer University

John Wiley & Sons, Inc.

CHAPTER 10
PLANT ASSETS, NATURAL RESOURCES, AND INTANGIBLE ASSETS

After studying this chapter, you should be able to:

1 Describe the application of the cost principle to plant assets.

2 Explain the concept of depreciation.

3 Compute periodic depreciation using different methods.

4 Describe the procedure for revising periodic depreciation.

5 Distinguish between revenue and capital expenditures and explain the entries for these expenditures.

CHAPTER 10
PLANT ASSETS, NATURAL RESOURCES, AND INTANGIBLE ASSETS

After studying this chapter, you should be able to:

6 Explain how to account for the disposal of a plant asset through retirement, sale, or exchange.

7 Identify the basic accounting issues related to natural resources.

8 Contrast the accounting for intangible assets with the accounting for plant assets.

9 Indicate how plant assets, natural resources, and intangible assets are reported and analyzed.

PREVIEW OF CHAPTER 10

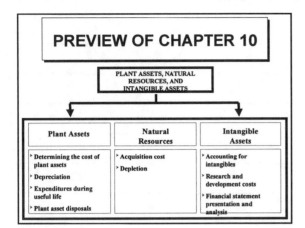

PLANT ASSETS, NATURAL RESOURCES, AND INTANGIBLE ASSETS

Plant Assets	Natural Resources	Intangible Assets
› Determining the cost of plant assets	› Acquisition cost	› Accounting for intangibles
› Depreciation	› Depletion	› Research and development costs
› Expenditures during useful life		› Financial statement presentation and analysis
› Plant asset disposals		

PLANT ASSETS

- Plant assets are tangible resources that are used in the operations of a business and are not intended for sale to customers.
- Plant assets are subdivided into four classes:
  1 Land
  2 Land improvements
  3 Buildings
  4 Equipment

STUDY OBJECTIVE 1

1 Describe the application of the cost principle to plant assets.

DETERMINING THE COST OF PLANT ASSETS

- Plant assets are recorded at cost in accordance with the cost principle.
- Cost consists of all expenditures necessary to acquire the asset and make it ready for its intended use.
- These costs include purchase price, freight costs, and installation costs.
- Expenditures that are not necessary should be recorded as expenses, losses, or other assets.

MEASUREMENT OF PLANT ASSET COST

- Cost is measured by the cash paid in a cash transaction or by the cash equivalent price when noncash assets are used in payment.
- The cash equivalent price is equal to the fair market value of the asset given up or the fair market value of the asset received, whichever is more clearly determinable.

LAND

- The cost of Land includes:
  1 cash purchase price
  2 closing costs such as title and attorney's fees
  3 real estate brokers' commissions
  4 accrued property taxes and other liens on the land assumed by the purchaser.
- All necessary costs incurred in making land ready for its intended use are debited to the Land account.

ILLUSTRATION 10-2
COMPUTATION OF COST OF LAND

Sometimes purchased land has a building on it that must be removed to make the site suitable for construction of a new building. In this case, all demolition and removal costs less any proceeds from salvaged materials are chargeable to the Land account.

Land	
Cash price of property	$ 100,000
Net removal cost of warehouse	6,000
Attorney's fee	1,000
Real estate broker's commission	8,000
Cost of land	$ 115,000

LAND IMPROVEMENTS

The cost of land improvements includes all expenditures necessary to make the improvements ready for their intended use such as:

1 parking lots,

2 fencing, and

3 lighting.

Lighting

Parking Lot

BUILDINGS

- The cost of buildings includes all necessary expenditures relating to the purchase or construction of a building:
- When a building is purchased, such costs include the purchase price, closing costs, and real estate broker's commission.
- Costs to make the building ready for its intended use consist of expenditures for remodeling and replacing or repairing the roof, floors, wiring, and plumbing.
- When a new building is constructed, cost consists of the contract price plus payments for architects' fees, building permits, interest payments during construction, and excavation costs.

EQUIPMENT

- The cost of equipment consists of the cash purchase price, sales taxes, freight charges, and insurance paid by the purchaser during transit.
- Cost includes all expenditures required in assembling, installing, and testing the unit.
- Recurring costs such as licenses and insurance are expensed as incurred.

ILLUSTRATION 10-3
COMPUTATION OF COST OF
DELIVERY TRUCK

The cost of equipment consists of the cash purchase price, sales taxes, freight charges, and insurance during transit paid by the purchaser. It also includes expenditures required in assembling, installing, and testing the unit. However, motor vehicle licenses and accident insurance on company cars and trucks are expensed as incurred, since they represent annual recurring that do not benefit future periods.

Delivery Truck	
Cash price	$ 22,000
Sales taxes	1,320
Painting and lettering	500
Cost of delivery truck	$ 23,820

ENTRY TO RECORD
PURCHASE OF TRUCK

Delivery Truck	
Cash price	$ 22,000
Sales taxes	1,320
Painting and lettering	500
Cost of delivery truck	$ 23,820

The entry to record the cost of the delivery truck and related expenditures is as follows:

Account Titles and Explanation	Debit	Credit
Delivery Truck	23,820	
License Expense	80	
Prepaid Insurance	1,600	
Cash		25,500
(To record purchase of delivery truck and related expenditures)		

ENTRY TO RECORD PURCHASE OF MACHINERY

Factory Machinery

Cash price	$ 50,000
Sales taxes	3,000
Insurance during shipping	500
Installation and testing	1,000
Cost of factory machinery	$ 54,500

The summary entry to record the cost of the factory machinery and related expenditures is as follows:

Account Titles and Explanation	Debit	Credit
Factory Machinery	54,500	
Cash		54,500
(To record purchase of factory machine)		

STUDY OBJECTIVE 2

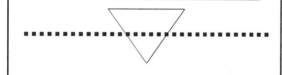

2 Explain the concept of depreciation.

DEPRECIATION

- Depreciation is the process of allocating to expense the cost of a plant asset over its useful (service) life in a rational and systematic manner.
- Cost allocation is designed to provide for the proper matching of expenses with revenues in accordance with the matching principle.
- During an asset's life, its usefulness may decline because of wear and tear or obsolescence.
- Recognition of depreciation does not result in the accumulation of cash for the replacement of the asset.
- Land is the only plant asset that is not depreciated.

FACTORS IN COMPUTING DEPRECIATION

THREE FACTORS THAT AFFECT THE COMPUTATION OF DEPRECIATION ARE:

1 Cost: all expenditures necesary to acquire the asset and make it ready for intended use.

2 Useful life: estimate of the expected life based on need for repair, service life, and vulnerability to obsolescence.

3 Salvage value: estimate of the asset's value at the end of its useful life.

STUDY OBJECTIVE 3

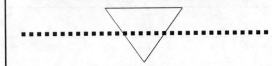

3 Compute periodic depreciation using different methods.

ILLUSTRATION 10-7
USE OF DEPRECIATION METHODS IN MAJOR U.S. COMPANIES

Three methods of recognizing depreciation are: 1 Straight-line, 2 Units of activity, and 3 Declining-balance. Each method is acceptable under generally accepted accounting principles. Management selects the method that is appropriate in the circumstances. Once a method is chosen, it should be applied consistently.

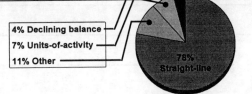

4% Declining balance
7% Units-of-activity
11% Other
78% Straight-line

ILLUSTRATION 10-8
DELIVERY TRUCK DATA

- To facilitate the comparison of the 3 depreciation methods, we will base all computations on the following data applicable to a small delivery truck purchased by Barb's Florists on June 1, 1999.

Cost	$13,00
Expected salvage value	$1,00
Estimated useful life in years	
Estimated useful life in miles	100,00

STRAIGHT-LINE

- Under the straight-line method, Depreciation is the same for each year of the asset's useful life.
- It is measured solely by the passage of time.
- In order to computer depreciation expense, it is necessary to determin depreciable cost.
- Depreciable cost is the total amount subject to depreciation and is computed as follows:
- Cost of asset - salvage value

ILLUSTRATION 10-9
FORMULA FOR STRAIGHT-LINE METHOD

The formula for computing annual depreciation expense is:
Depreciable Cost / Useful Life (in years) = Depreciation Expense

Cost	—	Salvage Value	$=$	Depreciable Cost
$13,000	-	$1,000	=	$12,000

Depreciable Cost	÷	Useful Life (in Years)	$=$	Depreciation Expense
$12,000	÷	5	=	$2,400

UNITS-OF-ACTIVITY

- Under the units-of-activity method, service life is expressed in terms of the total units of production or expected use from the asset, rather than time.
- The formulas for computing depreciation expense are:
- Depreciable Cost Total Units of Activity = Depreciation Cost per Unit
- Depreciation Cost per Unit X Units of Activity During the Year = Depreciation Expense
- In using this method, it is often difficult to make a reasonable estimate of total activity.
- When the productivity of an asset varies significantly from one period to another, this method results in the best matching of expenses with revenues.

ILLUSTRATION 10-11
FORMULA FOR UNITS-OF-ACTIVITY METHOD

To use the units-of-activity method, 1 the total units of activity for the entire useful life are estimated, 2 the amount is divided into depreciable cost to determine the depreciation cost per unit, and 3 the depreciation cost per unit is then applied to the units of activity during the year to determine the annual depreciation.

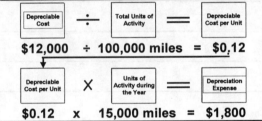

Depreciable Cost	÷	Total Units of Activity	=	Depreciable Cost per Unit
$12,000	÷	100,000 miles	=	$0.12

Depreciable Cost per Unit	X	Units of Activity during the Year	=	Depreciation Expense
$0.12	x	15,000 miles	=	$1,800

DECLINING-BALANCE

- The declining-balance method produces a decreasing annual depreciation expense over the useful life of the asset.
- The calculation of periodic depreciation is based on a declining book value (cost less accumulated depreciation) of the asset.
- Annual depreciation expense is calculated by multiplying the book value at the beginning of the year by the declining-balance depreciation rate.
- The depreciation rate remains constant from year to year, but the book value to which the rate is applied declines each year.

DECLINING-BALANCE

- The book value for the first year is the cost of the asset since accumulated depreciation has a zero balance at the beginning of the asset's useful life.
- In subsequent years, book value is the difference between cost and accumulated depreciation at the beginning of the year.
- The formula for computing depreciation expense is:
  Book Value at Beginning of Year X Declining Balance Rate = Depreciation Expense
- This method is compatible with the matching principle because the higher depreciation in early years is matched with the higher benefits received in these years.

ILLUSTRATION 10-13
FORMULA FOR DECLINING-BALANCE METHOD

Unlike the other depreciation methods, salvage value is ignored in determining the amount to which the declining balance rate is applied.

A common application of the declining-balance method is the double-declining-balance method, in which the declining-balance rate is double the straight-line rate.

If Barb's Florists uses the double-declining-balance method, the depreciation is 40% (2 X the straight-line rate of 20%).

Depreciable Cost per Unit	X	Units of Activity during the Year	=	Depreciation Expense
$13,000	x	40%	=	$5,200

STUDY OBJECTIVE 4

4 Describe the procedure for revising periodic depreciation.

REVISING PERIODIC DEPRECIATION

- If wear and tear or obsolescence indicate that annual depreciation is inadequate or excessive, a change in the periodic amount should be made.

- When a change is made,

  1 there is no correction of previously recorded depreciation expense and

  2 depreciation expense for current and future years is revised.

- To determine the new annual depreciation expense, the depreciable cost at the time of the revision is divided by the remaining useful life.

ILLUSTRATION 10-17
REVISED DEPRECIATION COMPUTATION

Barb's Florists decides on January 1, 2002 to extend the useful life of the truck one year because of its excellent condition. The company has used the straight-line method to depreciate the asset to date, and book value is $5,800 ($13,000 - $7,200). The new annual depreciation is $1,600, calculated as follows:

Book value, 1/1/02	$ 5,800
Less: Salvage value	1,000
Depreciable cost	$ 4,800
Remaining useful life	3 years (2002-2004)
Revised annual depreciation ($4,800 ÷ 3)	$ 1,600

STUDY OBJECTIVE 5

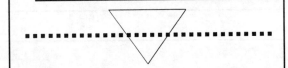

5 Distinguish between revenue and capital expenditures and explain the entries for these expenditures.

EXPENDITURES DURING USEFUL LIFE

- Ordinary repairs are expenditures to maintain the operating efficiency and expected productive life of the plant asset.
- They are debited to Repairs Expense as incurred and are often referred to as revenue expenditures.
- Additions and improvements are costs incurred to increase the operating efficiency, productive capacity, or expected useful life of the plant asset.
  1 Expenditures are usually material in amount and occur infrequently during the period of ownership.
  2 Since additions and improvements increase the company's investment in productive facilities, they are debits to the plant asset affected, and are referred to as capital expenditures .

STUDY OBJECTIVE 6

6 Explain how to account for the disposal of a plant asset through retirement, sale, or exchange.

PLANT ASSET DISPOSALS

- Disposal by retirement: the plant asset is scrapped or discarded.
- Eliminate the book value of the plant asset at the date of sale by debiting Accumulated Depreciation and crediting the asset account for its cost.
- Debit Cash to record the cash proceeds from the sale.
- Compute gain or loss.
- If the cash proceeds are greater than the book value, recognize a gain by crediting Gain on Disposal for the difference.
- If the cash proceeds are less than the book value, recognize a loss by debiting Loss on Disposal for the difference.

GAIN ON DISPOSAL

On July 1, 1999, Wright Company sells office furniture for $16,000 cash. Original cost was $60,000 and as of January 1, 1999, had accumulated depreciation of $41,000. Depreciation for the first 6 months of 1999 is $8,000. The entry to record depreciation expense and update accumulated depreciation to July 1 is as follows:

Date	Account Titles and Explanation	Debit	Credit
1999 July 1	Depreciation Expense	8,000	
	Accumulated Depreciation — Office Furniture		8,000
	(To record depreciation expense for the first six months of 1999)		

ILLUSTRATION 10-19
GAIN ON DISPOSAL

After the accumulated depreciation is updated, a gain on disposal of $5,000 is calculated:

Cost of office furniture	$ 60,000
Less: Accumulated depreciation ($41,000 + $8,000)	49,000
Book value at date of disposal	11,000
Proceeds from sale	16,000
Gain on disposal	$ 5,000

The entry to record the sale and the gain on disposal is as follows:

Date	Account Titles and Explanation	Debit	Credit
1999 July 1	Cash	16,000	
	Accumulated Depreciation — Office Furniture	49,000	
	Office Furniture		60,000
	Gain on Disposal		5,000
	(To record sale of office furniture at a gain)		

ILLUSTRATION 10-20
LOSS ON DISPOSAL

Instead of the selling the office furniture for $16,000, Wright sells it for $9,000. In this case, a loss of $2,000 is calculated:

Cost of office furniture	$ 60,000
Less: Accumulated depreciation ($41,000 + $8,000)	49,000
Book value at date of disposal	11,000
Proceeds from sale	9,000
Loss on disposal	$ 2,000

The entry to record the sale and the loss on disposal is as follows:

Date	Account Titles and Explanation	Debit	Credit
1999 July 1	Cash	9,000	
	Accumulated Depreciation — Office Furniture	49,000	
	Loss on Disposal	2,000	
	Office Furniture		60,000
	(To record sale of office furniture at a loss)		

EXCHANGES OF PLANT ASSETS

● Exchanges of plant assets can be for similar or dissimilar assets.

● An exchange of similar plant assets involves assets of the same type.

● In an exchange of similar assets, the new asset performs the same function as the old asset.

● In exchanges of similar assets, it is necessary to determine

1 the cost of the asset acquired and

2 the gain or loss on the asset given up.

LOSS TREATMENT

● Losses on the exchange of similar assets are recognized immediately.

● The cost of the new asset received is equal to the fair market value of the old asset exchanged plus any cash or other consideration given up.

● A loss results when the book value is greater than the fair market value of the asset given up.

ILLUSTRATION 10-21
COMPUTATION OF COST OF NEW OFFICE EQUIPMENT

Roland Company exchanges old office equipment for new similar office equipment. The book value of the old office equipment is $26,000 ($70,000 cost less $44,000 accumulated depreciation), AND its fair market value is $10,000, and $81,000 of cash is paid. The cost of the new office equipment, $91,000, is calculated as follows:

Fair market value of old office equipment	$ 10,000
Cash	81,000
Cost of new office equipment	$ 91,000

ILLUSTRATION 10-22
COMPUTATION OF LOSS ON DISPOSAL

Through this exchange, a loss on disposal of $16,000 is incurred. A loss results when the book value is greater than the fair market value of the asset given up. The calculation is as follows:

Book value of old office equipment ($70,000 — $44,000)	$ 26,000
Fair market value of old office equipment	10,000
Loss on disposal	$ 16,000

In recording the exchange at a loss it is necessary to 1 eliminate the book value of the asset given up, 2 record the cost of the asset acquired, and 3 recognize the loss on disposal.

Account Titles and Explanation	Debit	Credit
Office Equipment (new)	91,000	
Accumulated Depreciation — Office Equipment (old)	44,000	
Loss on Disposal	16,000	
Office Equipment (old)		70,000
Cash		81,000
(To record exchange of old office equipment for similar new equipment)		

GAIN TREATMENT

- Gains on exchange of similar assets are not recognized immediately. Instead, they are deferred and reduce the cost basis of the new asset.
- The cost of the new asset received is equal to the fair market value of the old asset exchanged plus any cash or other consideration given up.
- A gain results when the fair market value is greater than the book value of the asset given up.

ILLUSTRATION 10-23
COST OF NEW EQUIPMENT
(BEFORE DEFERRAL OF GAIN)

Mark's Express Delivery exchanges old delivery equipment plus $3,000 cash for new delivery equipment. The book value of the old delivery equipment is $12,000 ($40,000 cost less $28,000 accumulated depreciation), its fair market value is $19,000. The cost of the new delivery equipment, $22,000, is calculated as follows:

Fair market value of old delivery equipment	$ 19,000
Cash	3,000
Cost of new delivery equipment (before deferral of gain)	$ 22,000

ILLUSTRATION 10-24
COMPUTATION OF GAIN ON DISPOSAL

For Mark's Express Delivery, there is a gain of $7,000, calculated as follows, on the disposal:

Fair market value of old delivery equipment	$ 19,000
Book value of old delivery equipment ($40,000 – $28,000)	12,000
Gain on disposal	$ 7,000

ILLUSTRATION 10-25
COST OF NEW DELIVERY EQUIPMENT
(AFTER DEFERRAL OF GAIN)

The $7,000 gain on disposal is then offset against the $22,000 cost of the new delivery equipment. The result is a $15,000 cost of the new delivery equipment, after deferral of the gain.

Cost of new delivery equipment (before deferral of gain)	$ 22,000
Less: Gain on disposal	7,000
Cost of new delivery equipment (after deferral of gain)	$ 15,000

The entry to record the exchange is as follows:

Account Titles and Explanation	Debit	Credit
Delivery Equipment (new)	15,000	
Accumulated Depreciation — Delivery Equipment (old)	28,000	
Delivery Equipment (old)		40,000
Cash		3,000
(To record exchange of old delivery equipment for similar new delivery equipment)		

ILLUSTRATION 10-26
ACCOUNTING RULES FOR
PLANT EXCHANGES

Type of Event	Recognition
Loss	Recognize immediately by debiting Loss on Disposal
Gain	Defer and reduce cost of new asset

STUDY OBJECTIVE 7

7 Identify the basic accounting issues related to natural resources.

NATURAL RESOURCES

- Natural resources consist of standing timber and underground deposits of oil, gas, and minerals.
- Natural resources, frequently called wasting assets, have two distinguishing characteristics:
  1 They are physically extracted in operations.
  2 They are replaceable only by an act of nature.

ACQUISITION COST

- The acquisition cost of a natural resource is the cash or cash equivalent price necessary to acquire the resource and prepare it for its intended use.
- If the resource is already discovered, cost is the price paid for the property.
- If exploration is involved, the problem is whether or not to capitalize successful as well as unsuccessful explorations.

ACQUISITION COST

- Under the full-cost approach, both successful and unsuccessful explorations are capitalized, and the costs are written off to expense over the useful life of the successful wells.

- Under the successful efforts approach, only the costs of successful explorations are capitalized and the costs written off to expense over their useful life.

DEPLETION

- The process of allocating the cost of natural resources to expense in a rational and systematic manner over the resource's useful life is called depletion.

- The units-of-activity method is generally used to compute depletion, because periodic depletion generally is a function of the units extracted during the year.

ILLUSTRATION 10-27
FORMULA TO COMPUTE DEPLETION EXPENSE

| Total Cost minus Salvage Value | ÷ | Total Estimated Units | = | Depletion Cost per Unit |

| Depletion Cost per Unit | X | Number of Units Extracted and Sold | = | Depletion Expense |

Helpful hint: The computation for depletion is similar to the computation for depreciation using the units-of-activity method.

RECORDING DEPLETION

The Lane Coal Company invests $5 million in a mine estimated to have 10 million tons of coal and no salvage value. In the first year, 800,000 tons of coal are extracted and sold. Using the formulas, the calculations are as follows:

$5,000,000 ÷ 10,000,000 = $.50 depletion cost per ton
$.50 X 800,000 = $400,000 depletion expense

The entry to record depletion expense for the first year of operations is as follows:

Date	Account Titles and Explanation	Debit	Credit
Dec. 31	Depletion Expense	400,000	
	Accumulated Depletion		400,000
	(To record depletion expense on coal deposits)		

ILLUSTRATION 10-28
BALANCE SHEET
PRESENTATION OF DEPLETION

Accumulated Depletion, a contra asset account similar to accumulated depreciation, is deducted from the cost of the natural resource in the balance sheet as follows:

Lane Coal Company
Balance Sheet (partial)

Coal mine	$5,000,000	
Less: Accumulated depletion	400,000	$4,600,000

STUDY OBJECTIVE 8

8 Contrast the accounting for intangible assets with the accounting for plant assets.

INTANGIBLE ASSETS

- Intangible assets are rights, privileges, and competitive advantages that result from the ownership of long lived assets that do not possess physical substance.
- Intangibles may arise from government grants, acquisition of another business, and private monopolistic arrangements.

ACCOUNTING FOR INTANGIBLE ASSETS

- In general, accounting for intangible assets parallels the accounting for plant assets.
- Intangible assets are:
  1 recorded at cost;
  2 written off over useful life in a rational and systematic manner; and
  3 at disposal, book value is eliminated and gain or loss, if any, is recorded.

ACCOUNTING FOR INTANGIBLE ASSETS

- Differences between the accounting for intangible assets and the accounting for plant assets include:
- The systematic write-off of an intangible asset is referred to as amortization.
- To record amortization, Amortization Expense is debited and the specific intangible asset is credited.
- The amortization period cannot be longer than 40 years.
- Amortization is typically computed on a straight-line basis.

PATENTS

- A patent is an exclusive right issued by the United States Patent Office that enables the recipient to manufacture, sell, or otherwise control his or her invention for a period of 17 years from the date of grant.
- The initial cost of a patent is the cash or cash equivalent price paid when the patent is acquired.
- Legal costs incurred in successfully defending the patent are added to the Patent account and amortized over the remaining useful life of the patent.
- The cost of the patent should be amortized over its 17-year legal life or its useful life, whichever is shorter.

RECORDING PATENTS

National Labs purchases a patent at a cost of $60,000. If the useful life of the patent is 8 years, the annual amortization expense is $7,500 ($56,000 ÷ 8).
Patent Expense is classified as an operating expense in the income statement. The entry to record the annual patent amortization is:

Date	Account Titles and Explanation	Debit	Credit
Dec. 31	Patent Expense	7,500	
	Patents		7,500
	(To record patent amortization)		

COPYRIGHTS

- Copyrights are granted by the federal government, giving the owner the exclusive right to reproduce and sell an artistic or published work.
- Copyrights extend for the life of the creator plus 50 years.
- The cost of a copyright consists of the cost of acquiring and defending it.

TRADEMARKS AND TRADE NAMES

- A trademark or trade name is a word, phrase, jingle, or symbol that distinguishes or identifies a particular enterprise or product.
- If the trademark or trade name is purchased, the cost is the purchase price. **TM**
- If it is developed by a company, the cost includes attorney's fees, registration fees, design costs and successful legal defense fees.
- They are amortized over the shorter of useful life or 40 years.

FRANCHISES AND LICENSES

- A franchise is a contractual arrangement under which the franchisor grants the franchisee the right to sell certain products, to render specific services, or to use certain trademarks or trade names, usually within a designated geographical area.
- Another type of franchise, commonly referred to as a license or permit, is entered into between a governmental body and a business enterprise and permits the enterprise to use public property in performing its services.

GOODWILL

- Goodwill is the value of all favorable attributes that relate to a business enterprise.
- These attributes may include exceptional management, desirable location, good customer relations and skilled employees.
- Goodwill cannot be sold individually in the marketplace; it can be identified only with the business as a whole.

GOODWILL

- Goodwill is recorded only when there is an exchange transaction that involves the purchase of an entire business.
- When an entire business is purchased, goodwill is the excess of cost over the fair market value of the net assets (assets less liabilities) acquired.
- Goodwill is written off over its useful life not to exceed forty years.

RESEARCH AND DEVELOPMENT COSTS

- Research and development costs pertain to expenditures incurred to develop new products and processes.
- These costs are not intangible costs, but are usually recorded as an expense when incurred.

STUDY OBJECTIVE 9

9 Indicate how plant assets, natural resources and intangible assets are reported and analyze.

FINANCIAL STATEMENT PRESENTATION

- Usually plant assets and natural resources are combined under Property, Plant, and Equipment, and intangibles are shown separately under Intangible Assets.

- Major classes of assets, such as land, buildings, and equipment, and accumulated depreciation by major classes or in total should be disclosed.

- The depreciation and amortization methods used should be described and the amount of depreciation and amortization expense for the period disclosed.

ILLUSTRATION 10-29
KELLOGG'S PRESENTATION OF PROPERTY, PLANT, AND EQUIPMENT, AND INTANGIBLES

The financial statement presentation of property, plant, and equipment by Kellogg Company in its 1997 balance sheet is quite brief, as shown below:

Kellogg Company Balance Sheet (partial) December 31 (in millions)		
	1997	1996
Property, net	$2,773.33	$2,932.9
Other assets	636.6	588.5

The notes to Kellogg's financial statements present greater details, namely, that "Other Assets" contains goodwill of $194.7 million and other intangibles of $191.2 million.

ILLUSTRATION 10-30
PRESENTATION OF PROPERTY, PLANT, AND EQUIPMENT AND INTANGIBLE ASSETS

A more comprehensive presentation of property, plant, and equipment is excerpted from the balance sheet of Owens-Illinois and shown below.

OWENS-ILLINOIS, INC. Balance Sheet - Partial (In millions of dollars)		
Property, plant, and equipment		
Timberlands, at cost, less accumulated depletion		$ 95.4
Buildings and equipment, at cost	$ 2,207.1	
Less: Accumulated depreciation	1,229.0	978.1
Total property, plant, and equipment		$ 1,073.5
Intangibles		
Patents		410.0
Total		$ 1,483.5

Chapter 11
Current Liabilities and Payroll Accounting

Accounting Principles, 5e
Weygandt, Kieso, & Kimmel

Prepared by
Marianne Bradford
The University of Tennessee
Gregory K. Lowry
Mercer University

John Wiley & Sons, Inc.

CHAPTER 11
CURRENT LIABILITIES AND PAYROLL ACCOUNTING

After studying this chapter, you should be able to:

1 Explain a current liability and identify the major types of current liabilities.
2 Describe the accounting for notes payable.
3 Explain the accounting for other current liabilities.
4 Explain the methods for the financial statement presentation and analysis of current liabilities.
5 Describe the accounting and disclosure requirements for contingent liabilities.

CHAPTER 11
CURRENT LIABILITIES AND PAYROLL ACCOUNTING

After studying this chapter, you should be able to:

6 Discuss the objectives of internal control for payroll.
7 Compute and record the payroll for a pay period.
8 Describe and record employer payroll taxes.
9 Identify additional fringe benefits associated with employee compensation.

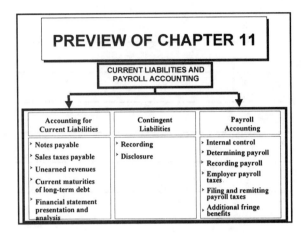

PREVIEW OF CHAPTER 11

CURRENT LIABILITIES AND PAYROLL ACCOUNTING

Accounting for Current Liabilities	Contingent Liabilities	Payroll Accounting
› Notes payable	› Recording	› Internal control
› Sales taxes payable	› Disclosure	› Determining payroll
› Unearned revenues		› Recording payroll
› Current maturities of long-term debt		› Employer payroll taxes
› Financial statement presentation and analysis		› Filing and remitting payroll taxes
		› Additional fringe benefits

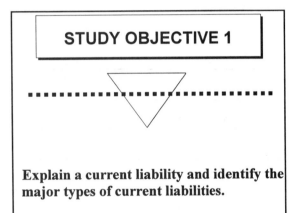

STUDY OBJECTIVE 1

Explain a current liability and identify the major types of current liabilities.

ACCOUNTING FOR CURRENT LIABILITIES

■ A Current Liability is a debt that can reasonably be expected to be paid:

1 from existing current assets or in the creation of other current liabilities and

2 within one year or the operating cycle, whichever is longer.

■ Current liabilities include:

1 Notes Payable

2 Accounts Payable

3 Unearned Revenues

4 Accrued Liabilities

STUDY OBJECTIVE 2

Describe the accounting for notes payable.

NOTES PAYABLE

- Notes Payable are obligations in the form of written promissory notes that usually require the borrower to pay interest.
- Notes payable may be used instead of accounts payable because it supplies documentation of the obligation in case legal remedies are needed to collect the debt.
- Notes due for payment within one year of the balance sheet date are usually classified as current liabilities.

NOTES PAYABLE

GENERAL JOURNAL			
Mar. 1	Cash	100,000	
	Notes Payable		100,000
	(To record issuance of 12%, 4-month note to First National Bank		

When an interest-bearing note is issued, the assets received generally equal the face value of the note. Assume First National Bank agrees to lend $100,000 on March 1, 1999, if Cole Williams Co. signs a $100,000, 12%, 4-month note. Cash is debited and Notes Payable is credited.

NOTES PAYABLE

GENERAL JOURNAL

June 30	Interest Expense	4,000	
	Interest Payable		4,000
	(To accrue interest for 4 months on First National Bank note)		

Interest accrues over the life of the note and must be recorded periodically. If Cole Williams Co. prepares financial statements semiannually, an adjusting entry is required to recognize interest expense and interest payable of $4,000 at June 30.

Illustration 11-1
Formula for computing interest

The formula for computing interest and its application to Cole Williams Co. are shown below:

Face Value of Note	Annual Interest Rate	Time in Terms of One Year	Interest
$100,000 x	12% x	4/12 =	$4,000

NOTES PAYABLE

GENERAL JOURNAL

July 1	Notes Payable	100,000	
	Interest Payable	4,000	
	Cash		104,000
	(To record payment of First National Bank interest-bearing note and accrued at maturity)		

At maturity, Notes Payable is debited for the face value of the note, Interest Payable is debited for the amount of accrued interest, and Cash is credited for the maturity value of the note.

STUDY OBJECTIVE 3

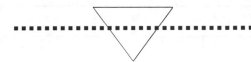

3 Explain the accounting for other current liabilities.

SALES TAXES PAYABLE

- Sales tax is expressed as a stated percentage of the sales price on goods sold to customers by a retailer.
- The retailer (or selling company) collects the tax from the customer when the sale occurs, and periodically (usually monthly) remits the collections to the state's department of revenue.
- Thus, the retailer serves as a collection agent for the taxing authority.

SALES TAXES PAYABLE

GENERAL JOURNAL		
Mar. 25	Cash	10,600	
	Sales		10,000
	Sales Taxes Payable		600
	(To record daily sales and sales taxes)		

Cash register readings are used to credit Sales and Sales Taxes Payable. If on March 25th cash register readings for Cooley Grocery show sales of $10,000 and sales taxes of $600 (sales tax rate is 6%), the entry is a debit to Cash for the total, and a credit to Sales for the actual sales and Sales Taxes Payable for the amount of the sales tax.

SALES TAXES PAYABLE

- When sales taxes are not rung up separately on the cash register, total receipts are divided by 100% plus the sales tax percentage to determine the sales, and the difference is sales tax.
- If Cooley Grocery "rings up" total receipts, which are $10,600, and the sales tax percentage is 6%, we can figure sales as follows:

$10,600	÷	1.06	=	$10,000

UNEARNED REVENUES

- Unearned Revenues (advances from customers) occur when a company receives cash before a service is rendered.
- Examples are when an airline sells a ticket for future flights or when an attorney receives legal fees before work is done.

UNEARNED REVENUES

GENERAL JOURNAL			
Aug. 6	Cash	500,000	
	Unearned Football Ticket Revenue		500,000
	(To record sale of 10,000 season tickets)		

If Superior University sells 10,000 season football tickets at $50 each for its five-game home schedule, the entry for the sale of the tickets is a debit to Cash for the advance received, and a credit to Unearned Football Ticket Revenue, a current liability.

UNEARNED REVENUES

GENERAL JOURNAL

Sept 7	Unearned Football Ticket Revenue	100,000	
	Football Ticket Revenue		100,000
	(To record football ticket revenues earned)		

As each game is completed, the Unearned Football Ticket Revenue account is debited for 1/5 of the unearned revenue, and the earned revenue, Football Ticket Revenue, is credited.

Illustration 11-2
Unearned and earned revenue accounts

Shown below are specific unearned and earned revenue accounts used in selected types of businesses.

	Account Title	
Type of business	Unearned Revenue	Earned Revenue
Airline	Unearned Passenger Ticket Revenue	Passenger Revenue
Magazine publisher	Unearned Subscription Revenue	Subscription Revenue
Hotel	Unearned Rental Revenue	Rental Revenue

CURRENT MATURITIES OF LONG-TERM DEBT

- Another item classified as a current liability is current maturities of long-term debt.
- Current maturities of long-term debt are often identified on the balance sheet as long-term debt due within one year.

STUDY OBJECTIVE 4

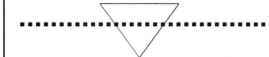

4 **Explain the methods for the financial statement presentation and analysis of current liabilities.**

FINANCIAL STATEMENT PRESENTATION

■ Current liabilities is the first category under liabilities on the balance sheet. Each of the principal types of current liabilities is listed separately.

■ Current liabilities are seldom listed in the order of maturity because of the varying maturity dates that may exist for specific obligations such as notes payable.

■ A more common method of presenting current liabilities is to list them by order of magnitude, with the largest obligations first.

■ However, many companies, as a matter of custom, show notes payable and accounts payable first regardless of amount.

■ The following slide is adapted from the balance sheet of **Kellogg Company**, and illustrates this practice.

ILLUSTRATION 11-3
BALANCE SHEET PRESENTATION
OF CURRENT LIABILITIES

KELLOGG COMPANY
Balance Sheet
December 31, 1999
(in millions)

ASSETS	
Current assets	$ 1,467.7
Property, plant and equipment (net)	2,773.3
Identifiable intangible assets and goodwill	636.6
Total Assets	$ 4,877.6
LIABILITIES AND STOCKHOLDERS' EQUITY	
Current liabilities	
Current maturities of long-term debt	$ 211.2
Notes payable	368.6
Accounts payable	328.0
Other current liabilities	749.5
Total current liabilities	1,657.3
Noncurrent liabilities	2,222.8
Shareholders' equity	997.5
Total liabilities and shareholders' equity	$ 4,877.6

Illustration 11-4
Working Capital formula and computation

The excess of current assets over current liabilities is working capital. The formula for the computation of Kellogg's working capital is shown below.

Current Assets	−	Current Liabilities	=	Working Capital

$ 1,467.7 - $ 1,657.3 = ($ 189.6)

Illustration 11-5
Current ratio and computation

The current ratio permits us to compare the liquidity of different sized companies and of a single company at different times. The current ratio for Kellogg Company is shown below.

Current Assets	/	Current Liabilities	=	Current Ratio

$1,467.7 / $1,657.3 = .89 : 1

STUDY OBJECTIVE 5

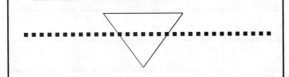

5 Describe the accounting and disclosure requirements for contingent liabilities.

CONTINGENT LIABILITIES

■ A contingent liability is a potential liability that may become an actual liability in the future.

■ The accounting guidelines require that:

1 If the contingency is probable and the amount can be reasonably estimated, the liability should be recorded in the accounts.

2 If the contingency is only reasonably possible, then it need be disclosed only in the notes accompanying the financial statements.

3 If the contingency is remote, it need not be recorded or disclosed.

PRODUCT WARRANTIES

■ Product warranties are an example of a contingent liability that should be record in the accounts.

■ They are recorded by estimating the cost of honoring product warranty contracts and expensing the amount in the period in which the sale occurs.

■ Warranty Expense is reported under selling expenses in the income statement, and estimating warranty liability is classified as a current liability on the balance sheet.

ILLUSTRATION 11-6
COMPUTATION OF ESTIMATED
PRODUCT WARRANTY LIABILITY

In 1999 Denson Manufacturing Company sells 10,000 washers and dryers at an average price of $600 each. The selling price includes a one-year warranty on parts. It is expected that 500 units (5%) will be defective and that warranty repair costs will average $80 per unit. The calculation of of estimated product costs on 1999 sales is as follows:

Number of units sold		10,000
Estimated rate of defective units	X	5%
Total estimated defective units		500
Average warranty repair cost	X $	80
Estimated product warranty liability		$ 40,000

ENTRIES TO RECORD WARRANTY COSTS

GENERAL JOURNAL

Dec. 31	Warranty Expense	40,000	
	Estimated Warranty Liability		40,000
	(To accrue estimated warranty costs)		

Denson Manufacturing Company makes the adjusting entry above to accrue the estimated warranty costs on 1999 sales. Warranty Expense is debited while Estimated Warranty Liability is credited for $40,000 at December 31.

ENTRIES TO RECORD WARRANTY COSTS

GENERAL JOURNAL

Jan. 1 – Dec. 31	Estimated Warranty Liability	24,000	
	Repair Parts		24,000
	(To record honoring of 300 warranty contracts on 1999 sales)		

Denson Manufacturing Company makes the $24,000 (300 X $80) summary entry above to record repair costs incurred in 1999 to honor warranty contracts on 1999 sales. Estimated Warranty Liability is debited while Repair Parts and Wages Payable are credited by December 31.

ENTRIES TO RECORD WARRANTY COSTS

GENERAL JOURNAL

Jan. 31	Estimated Warranty Liability	1,600	
	Repair Parts		1,600
	(To record honoring of 20 warranty contracts on 1999 sales)		

Denson Manufacturing Company replaced defective units in January 2000 for $1,600 (20 X $80) and made the summary entry above. Estimated Warranty Liability is debited while Repair Parts and Wages Payable are credited.

STUDY OBJECTIVE 6

6 Discuss the objectives of internal control for payroll.

PAYROLL ACCOUNTING

- The term payroll pertains to all salaries and wages paid to employees.
- Managerial, administrative, and sales personnel are generally paid salaries, which are often expressed in terms of a specified amount per month or year.
- Store clerks, factory employees and manual laborers are normally paid wages, which are based on a rate per hour.
- Payments made to professional individuals who are independent contractors are called fees.
- Government regulations relating to the payment and reporting of payroll taxes apply only to employees.

INTERNAL CONTROLS FOR PAYROLL

- The objectives of internal accounting control concerning payroll are:
  1 to safeguard company assets from unauthorized payrolls and
  2 to assure the accuracy and reliability of the accounting records pertaining to payrolls.
- 4 functions of payroll include:
  1 hiring employees,
  2 timekeeping,
  3 preparing the payroll, and
  4 paying the payroll.
- These functions should be assigned to different departments or individuals.

4 Functions of Payroll

HIRING EMPLOYEES

- The personnel department is responsible for ensuring the accuracy of the personnel authorization form.
- The personnel department is also responsible for authorizing:

  1 changes in pay rates during employment and

  2 termination of employment.

TIMEKEEPING

- Hourly employees are usually required to record time worked by "punching" a time clock – the time of arrival and departure are automatically recorded by the employee when he/she inserts a time card into the clock.
- In large companies, a supervisor or security guard often monitors time clock procedures, ensuring that each employee punches only one card.
- The employee's supervisor must:

  1 approve the hours shown by signing the time card at the end of the pay period and

  2 authorize any overtime hours for an employee.

PREPARING THE PAYROLL

The payroll department prepares the payroll on the basis of 2 sources of input:

1 personnel department authorizations and

2 approved time cards.

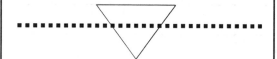

STUDY OBJECTIVE 7

7 Compute and record the payroll for a pay period.

DETERMINING AND PAYING THE PAYROLL

- Determining the payroll involves computing
  1 gross earnings,
  2 payroll deductions, and
  3 net pay.
- The payroll is paid by the treasurer's department.
  1 Payment by check minimizes the risk of loss from theft and
  2 the endorsed check provides proof of payment.

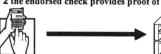

ILLUSTRATION 11-10
COMPUTATION OF TOTAL WAGES

- Gross earnings is the total compensation earned by an employee.
- There are 3 types of gross earnings: 1 wages, 2 salaries, and 3 bonuses.
- Total wages are determined by applying the hourly rate of pay to the hours worked.
- Most companies are required to pay a minimum of one and one-half times the regular hourly rate for overtime work.

Type of Pay	Hours	X	Rate	=	Gross Earnings
Regular	40	X	$ 12.00	=	$ 480.00
Overtime	4	X	18.00	=	72.00
Total wages					$ 552.00

PAYROLL DEDUCTIONS

- The difference between gross pay and the amount actually received is attributable to payroll deductions.
- Mandatory deductions consist of FICA taxes and income taxes.
- The employer collects these deductions and subsequently transfers them to the government and designated recipients.

ILLUSTRATION 11-11
PAYROLL DEDUCTIONS

FICA TAXES

- FICA taxes (or social security taxes) are designed to provide workers with supplemental retirement, employment disability, and medical benefits.
- The benefits are financed by a tax levied on employees' earnings.
- The tax rate and tax base for FICA taxes are set by Congress, and they are changed intermittently.

INCOME TAXES

■ Income Taxes are required to be withheld from employees each pay period and the amount is determined by 3 variables:

1 the employee's gross earnings;

2 the number of allowances claimed by the employee for herself or himself, his or her spouse, and other dependents; and

3 the length of the pay period.

■ To indicate to the Internal Revenue Service the number of allowances claimed, the employee must complete an Employee's Withholding Certificate (Form W-4).

VOLUNTARY DEDUCTIONS

■ Voluntary Deductions pertain to withholdings for charitable, retirement, and other purposes.

■ All voluntary deductions from gross earnings should be authorized in writing by the employee.

■ For purposes of illustration, the employee has the following voluntary deductions – including $10 for United Fund and $5 for union dues:

ILLUSTRATION 11-14
COMPUTATION OF NET PAY

Gross earnings		$ 552.00
Payroll deductions:		
FICA taxes	$ 44.16	
Federal income taxes	49.00	
State income taxes	11.04	
United Fund	10.00	
Union dues	5.00	119.20
Net pay		$ 432.80

Net Pay (or take-home pay) is determined by subtracting payroll deductions from gross earnings. Assuming an employee's wages are $552 each week, the employee will earn $28,704 for the year (52 weeks X $552). Thus, all earnings are subject to FICA taxes.

RECORDING THE PAYROLL

- The employee earnings record provides a cumulative record of each employee's gross earnings, deductions, and net pay during the year. This record is used by the employer in:

  1 determining when an employee has earned the maximum earnings subject to FICA taxes,

  2 filing state and federal payroll tax returns, and

  3 providing each employee with a statement of gross earnings and tax withholdings for the year.

- Many companies use a payroll register to accumulate the gross earnings, deductions, and net pay by employee for each period.

RECOGNIZING PAYROLL EXPENSES AND LIABILITIES

GENERAL JOURNAL			
Jan. 14	Office Salaries Expense	5,200.00	
	Wages Expense	12,010.00	
	FICA Taxes Payable		1,376.80
	Federal Income Taxes Payable		3,490.00
	State Income Taxes Payable		344.20
	United Fund Payable		421.50
	Union Dues Payable		115.00
	Salaries and Wages Payable		11,462.50
	(To record payroll for the week ending January 14)		

Academy Company records its payroll for the week ending January 14, 1999 with the journal entry above. Office Salaries Expense ($5,200) and Wages Payable ($12,010) are debited in total for $17,210 in gross earnings. Specific liability accounts are credited for the deductions made during the pay period. Salaries and Wages Payable is credited for $11,462.50 in net earnings.

RECORDING PAYMENT OF THE PAYROLL

GENERAL JOURNAL			
Jan. 14	Salaries and Wages Payable	11,462.50	
	Cash		11,462.50
	(To record payment of the payroll)		

The entry to record payment of the Academy Company payroll is a debit to Salaries and Wages Payable and a credit to Cash. When currency is used in payment, one check is prepared for the amount of net earnings ($11,462.50).

STUDY OBJECTIVE 8

8 Describe and record employer payroll taxes.

EMPLOYER PAYROLL TAXES

Payroll Tax Expense for businesses and educational institutions results from **3** taxes levied on employers by governmental agencies.

1 The employer must match each employee's FICA contribution – resulting in payroll tax expense to the employer.

2 Federal unemployment taxes (FUTA) provide benefits for a limited time period to employees who lose their jobs through no fault of their own. FUTA is a tax borne entirely by the employer.

3 State unemployment taxes (SUTA) also provide benefits to employees who lose their jobs and are borne entirely by the employer.

RECORDING EMPLOYER PAYROLL TAXES

The entry to record the payroll tax expense associated with the Academy Company payroll results in a debit to Payroll Tax Expense for $2,443.82, a credit to FICA Taxes Payable for $1,376.80 ($17,210 X 8%), a credit to FUTA Payable for $137.68 ($17,210 X 0.8%), and a credit to SUTA Payable for $929.34 ($17,210 X 5.4%).

GENERAL JOURNAL			
Jan. 14	Payroll Tax Expense	2,443.82	
	FICA Taxes Payable		1,376.80
	FUTA Payable		137.68
	SUTA Payable		929.34
	(To record employer's payroll taxes on January 14 payroll)		

FILING AND REMITTING PAYROLL TAXES

- Payroll tax returns preparation is the responsibility of the payroll department while payment of the taxes is made by the treasurer's department.
- FICA taxes and Federal income taxes (FIT) withheld are combined for reporting and remitting purposes.
- The taxes are reported quarterly – no later than one month after the close of each qurter.
- FUTA taxes are usually filed and remitted annually on or prior to January 31 of the subsequent year.
- SUTA taxes must be filed and paid by the end of the month following each quarter.
- The employer is required to provide each employee with a Wage and Tax Statement (Form W-2) by January 31 following the end of the calendar year.

STUDY OBJECTIVE 9

9 Identify additional fringe benefits associated with employee compensation.

ADDITIONAL FRINGE BENEFITS PAID ABSENCES

Employees often have rights to receive compensation for future absenses if certain conditions of employment are met. Such compensation may relate to 1 paid vacations, 2 sick pay benefits, and 3 paid holidays. A liability should be accrued for paid future absenses if 1 its payment is probable and 2 the amount can be reasonably estimated. Academy Company employees are entitled to one day's vacation for each month worked. If 30 employees earn an average of $110 per day in a given month, the accrual for vacation benefits for January is $3,300 ($110 X 30). The liability is recognized at January 31 by the following adjusting entry:

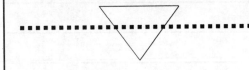

	GENERAL JOURNAL		
Jan. 31	Vacation Benefits Expense	3,300	
	Vacation Benefits Payable		3,300
	(To accrue vacation benefits expense)		

ADDITIONAL FRINGE BENEFITS
PAID ABSENCES

When vacation benefits are paid, Vacation Benefits Payable is debited and Cash is credited. If Academy Company pays such benefits for 10 employees in July, the journal entry to record the payment is for $1,100 ($110 X 10).

GENERAL JOURNAL			
July 31	Vacation Benefits Payable	1,100	
	Cash		1,100
	(To record payment of vacation benefits)		

POSTRETIREMENT BENEFITS

- Postretirement benefits consist of payments by employers to retired employees for:
  1 health care and life insurance and
  2 pensions
- Both types of postretirement benefits are accounted for on the accrual basis.

PENSION PLANS

- A pension plan is an agreement whereby an employer provides benefits to employees after they retire.
- 3 parties are generally involved in a pension plan.
  1 The employer sponsors the plan.
  2 The plan administrator receives the contributions, invests the pension assets, and makes the benefit payments.
  3 The retired employees receive the pension payments.

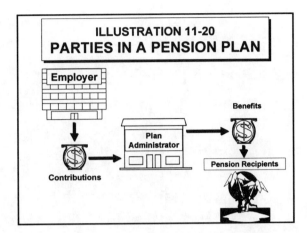

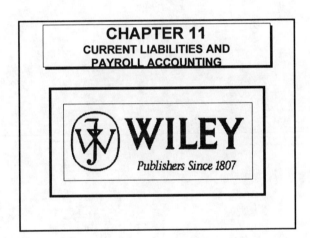

Accounting Principles, 5e
Weygandt, Kieso, & Kimmel

Prepared by
Marianne Bradford
The University of Tennessee
Gregory K. Lowry
Mercer University

John Wiley & Sons, Inc.

CHAPTER 12
ACCOUNTING PRINCIPLES

After studying this chapter, you should be able to:

1 Explain the meaning of generally accepted accounting principles and identify the key items of the conceptual framework.

2 Describe the basic objectives of financial reporting.

3 Discuss the qualitative characteristics of accounting information and elements of financial statements.

CHAPTER 12
ACCOUNTING PRINCIPLES

After studying this chapter, you should be able to:

4 Identify the basic assumptions used by accountants.

5 Identify the basic principles of accounting.

6 Identify the two constraints in accounting.

7 Explain the accounting principles used in international operations.

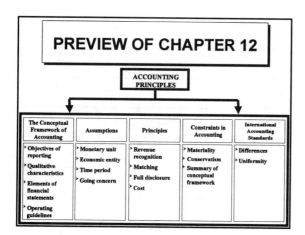

PREVIEW OF CHAPTER 12

ACCOUNTING PRINCIPLES

The Conceptual Framework of Accounting	Assumptions	Principles	Constraints in Accounting	International Accounting Standards
▸ Objectives of reporting	▸ Monetary unit	▸ Revenue recognition	▸ Materiality	▸ Differences
▸ Qualitative characteristics	▸ Economic entity	▸ Matching	▸ Conservatism	▸ Uniformity
▸ Elements of financial statements	▸ Time period	▸ Full disclosure	▸ Summary of conceptual framework	
▸ Operating guidelines	▸ Going concern	▸ Cost		

STUDY OBJECTIVE 1

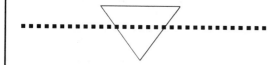

1 Explain the meaning of generally accepted accounting principles and identify the key items of the conceptual framework.

CONCEPTUAL FRAMEWORK OF ACCOUNTING

◆ Generally accepted accounting principles are a set of rules and practices that are recognized as a general guide for financial reporting purposes.

◆ Generally accepted means that these principles must have substantial authoritative support.

◆ This support usually comes from the Financial Accounting Standards Board (FASB) and Securities and Exchange Commission (SEC).

◆ The FASB has the responsibility for developing accounting principles in the United States.

FASB'S CONCEPTUAL FRAMEWORK

◆ The conceptual framework developed by the FASB serves as the basis for resolving accounting and reporting problems.

◆ The conceptual framework consists of:

1 objectives of financial reporting;

2 qualitative characteristics of accounting information;

3 elements of financial statements; and

4 Operating guidelines (assumptions, principles, and constraints).

STUDY OBJECTIVE 2

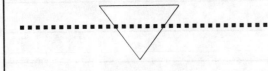

2 Describe the basic objectives of financial reporting.

OBJECTIVES OF FINANCIAL REPORTING

The FASB concluded that the objectives of financial reporting are to provide information that:

1 Is useful to those making investment and credit decisions.

2 Is helpful in assessing future cash flows.

3 Identifies the economic resources (assets), the claims to those resources (liabilities), and the changes in those resources and claims.

STUDY OBJECTIVE 3

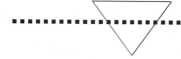

3 Discuss the qualitative characteristics of accounting information and elements of financial statements

---

QUALITATIVE CHARACTERISTICS OF ACCOUNTING INFORMATION

◆ The FASB concluded that the overriding criterion by which accounting choices should be judged is decision usefulness.

◆ To be useful, information should possess the following qualitative characteristics:

1 relevance,

2 reliability, and

3 comparability and consistency.

RELEVANCE

◆ Accounting information is relevant if it makes a difference in a decision.

◆ Relevant information helps users forecast future events (predictive value), or it confirms or corrects prior expectations (feedback value).

◆ Information must be available to decision makers before it loses its capacity to influence their decisions (timeliness).

RELIABILITY

◆ Reliability of information means that the information is free of error and bias; it can be depended on.

◆ To be reliable, accounting information must be verifiable – we must be able to prove that it is free of error and bias.

◆ The information must be a faithful representation of what it purports to be – it must be factual.

COMPARABILITY AND CONSISTENCY

◆ Comparability means that the information should be comparable with accounting information about other enterprises.

◆ Consistency means that the same accounting principles and methods should be used from year to year within a company.

ILLUSTRATION 12-1 QUALITATIVE CHARACTERISTICS OF ACCOUNTING INFORMATION

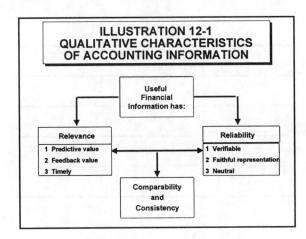

ILLUSTRATION 12-2
THE OPERATING GUIDELINES
OF ACCOUNTING

◆ Operating guidelines are classified as assumptions, principles, and constraints.

◆ Assumptions provide a foundation for the accounting process.

◆ Principles indicate how transactions and other economic events should be recorded.

◆ Constraints permit a company to modify generally accepted accounting principles without reducing the usefulness of the reported information.

Assumptions	Principals	Constraints
Monetary unit	Revenue recognition	Materiality
Economic entity	Matching	Conservatism
Time period	Full disclosure	
Going concern	Cost	

STUDY OBJECTIVE 4

4 Identify the basic assumptions used by accountants.

ASSUMPTIONS

1 The monetary unit assumption states that only transaction data capable of being expressed in terms of money should be included in the accounting records of the economic entity.

Example: employee satisfaction and percent of international employees are not transactions that should be included in the financial records.

Customer Satisfaction

Percentage of International Employees

Salaries paid

Should be included in accounting records

ASSUMPTIONS

2 The economic entity assumption states that economic events can be identified with a particular unit of accountability.

Example: BMW activities can be distinguished from those of other car manufacturers such as Mercedes.

ASSUMPTIONS

3 The time period assumption states that the economic life of a business can be divided into artificial time periods.

Example: months, quarters, and years

1997		1998	1999
QTR 1	JAN	FEB	MAR
QTR 2	APR	MAY	JUN
QTR 3	JUL	AUG	SEPT
QTR 4	OCT	NOV	DEC

GOING CONCERN ASSUMPTION

4 The going concern assumption assumes that the enterprise will continue in operation long enough to carry out its existing objectives.

Implications: depreciation and amortization are used, plant assets recorded at cost instead of liquidation value, items are labeled as fixed or long-term.

STUDY OBJECTIVE 5

5 Identify the basic principles of accounting.

PRINCIPLES
REVENUE RECOGNITION

◆ The revenue recognition principle dictates that revenue should be recognized in the accounting period in which it is earned.

◆ When a sale is involved, revenue is recognized at the point of sale.

PERCENTAGE-OF-COMPLETION METHOD OF REVENUE RECOGNITION

◆ In long-term construction contracts, recognition of revenue is usually required before the contract is completed.

◆ The percentage-of-completion method recognizes revenue and income on the basis of reasonable estimates of the project's progress toward completion.

◆ A project's progress toward completion is measured by comparing the costs incurred in a year to total estimated costs of the entire project.

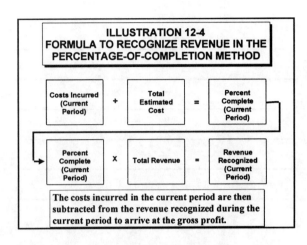

ILLUSTRATION 12-4
FORMULA TO RECOGNIZE REVENUE IN THE
PERCENTAGE-OF-COMPLETION METHOD

Costs Incurred (Current Period) + Total Estimated Cost = Percent Complete (Current Period)

Percent Complete (Current Period) X Total Revenue = Revenue Recognized (Current Period)

The costs incurred in the current period are then subtracted from the revenue recognized during the current period to arrive at the gross profit.

ILLUSTRATION 12-5
REVENUE RECOGNIZED
PERCENTAGE-OF-COMPLETION METHOD

Warrior Construction Co. has a contract to build a dam for $400 million. It will take 3 years (starting in 1997) at a construction cost of $360 million. Assume that Warrior incurs $54 million in 1997, $180 million in 1998, and $126 million in 1999 on the dam project. The portion of the $400 million of revenue recognized in each of the 3 years is shown below:

Year	Costs Incurred (Current Period)	+	Total Estimated Cost	=	Percent Complete (Current Period)	X	Total Revenue	=	Revenue Recognized (Current Period)
1997	$ 54,000,000	+	$ 360,000,000	=	15%	X	$ 400,000,000	=	$ 60,000,000
1998	180,000,000		360,000,000		50%		400,000,000		200,000,000
1999	126,000,000			Balance required to complete the contract					140,000,000
Totals	$ 360,000,000								$ 400,000,000

ILLUSTRATION 12-6
GROSS PROFIT RECOGNIZED
PERCENTAGE-OF-COMPLETION METHOD

The gross profit recognized each period for Warrior Construction Co. is as shown below. Since the application of the percentage-of-completion method involves some subjectivity, there is the possibility of error in determining the amount of revenue recognized and net income reported. To wait until completion would drastically distort the financial statements. If it is not possible to obtain dependable estimates of costs and progress, then the revenue should be recognized at the completion date and not by the percentage-of-completion method.

Year	Revenue Recognized (Current Period)	–	Actual Cost Incurred (Current Period)	=	Gross Profit Recognized (Current Period)
1997	$ 60,000,000	–	$ 54,000,000	=	$ 6,000,000
1998	200,000,000		180,000,000		20,000,000
1999	140,000,000		126,000,000		14,000,000
Totals	$ 400,000,000		$ 360,000,000		$ 40,000,000

INSTALLMENT METHOD OF REVENUE RECOGNITION

◆ Another basis for revenue recognition is the receipt of cash.

◆ The cash basis is generally used only when it is difficult to determine the revenue amount at the time of a credit sale because collection is so uncertain.

◆ The installment method, which uses the cash basis, is a popular approach to revenue recognition.

◆ Under the installment method gross profit is recognized in the period in which the cash is collected.

ILLUSTRATION 12-7 GROSS PROFIT FORMULA- INSTALLMENT METHOD

◆ Under installment method, each cash collection from a customer consists of

1 a partial recovery of the cost of goods sold and

2 partial gross profit from the sale.

◆ The formula to recognize gross profit is shown below.

| Cash Collections from Customers | X | Gross Profit Percentage | = | Gross Profit Recognized during the Period |

ILLUSTRATION 12-8 GROSS PROFIT RECOGNIZED INSTALLMENT METHOD

An Iowa farm machinery dealer had installment sales in its first year of operations of $600,000 and a cost of goods sold on installment of $420,000. Therefore, total gross profit is $180,000 ($600,000 - $420,000), and the gross profit percentage is 30% ($180,000 ÷ $600,000). The collections on the installment sales were: First year, $280,000 (down payments plus monthly payments), second year, $200,000, and third year, $120,000. The collections of cash and recognition of the gross profit are summarized below (ignoring interest charges).

Year	Cash Collected	X	Gross Profit Percentage	=	Gross Profit Recognized
1997	$ 280,000		30%		$ 84,000
1998	200,000		30%		60,000
1999	120,000		30%		36,000
Totals	$ 600,000				$ 180,000

PRINCIPLES
MATCHING (EXPENSE RECOGNITION)

◆ Expense recognition is traditionally tied to revenue recognition.

◆ This practice – referred to as the matching principle – dictates that expenses be matched with revenues in the period in which efforts are expended to generate revenues.

◆ To understand the various approaches for matching expenses and revenues on the income statement, it is necessary to examine the nature of expenses.

1 Expired costs are costs that will generate revenues only in the current period and are therefore reported as operating expenses on the income statement.

2 Unexpired costs are costs that will generate revenues in future accounting periods and are recognized as assets.

PRINCIPLES
MATCHING (EXPENSE RECOGNITION)

Unexpired costs become expenses in 2 ways:

1 Cost of goods sold – Costs carried as merchandise inventory are expensed as cost of goods sold in the period in which the sale occurs – so there is a direct matching of expenses with revenues.

2 Operating expenses – Unexpired costs become operating expenses through use or consumption or through the passage of time.

ILLUSTRATION 12-9
EXPENSE RECOGNITION PATTERN

Operating expenses contribute to the revenues of the period but their association with revenues is less direct than for cost of goods sold.

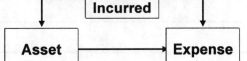

PRINCIPLES
FULL DISCLOSURE

◆ The full disclosure principle requires that circumstances and events that make a difference to financial statement users be disclosed.

◆ Compliance with the full disclosure principle is accomplished through

1 the data in the financial statements and

2 the notes that accompany the statements.

◆ A summary of significant accounting policies is usually the first note to the financial statements.

PRINCIPLES
COST

◆ The cost principle dictates that assets are recorded at their cost.

◆ Cost is used because it is both relevant and reliable.

1 Cost is relevant because if represents **a** the price paid, **b** the assets sacrificed, or **c** the commitment made at the date of acquisition.

2 Cost is reliable because it is **a)** objectively measurable, **b)** factual, and **c)** verifiable.

ILLUSTRATION 12-10
EXAMPLE OF CHANGING PRICES

Consider the data below in which 1980 prices are compared with 1999 expected prices, assuming average price increases of 6% and 12% per year.

	1980	1999	
Assumed price increase		6%	12%
Public college, yearly average cost	$ 3,350.00	$ 10,135.76	$ 28,852.75
Average taxi ride, New York City (before tip)	2.95	8.93	25.40
Slice of pizza	.85	1.97	5.60
First-class postage stamp	.15	.45	1.29
Run-of-the-mill suburban house, New York City	150,000.00	453,840.00	
McDonald's milk shake	.75	2.27	6.46

STUDY OBJECTIVE 6

6 Identify the two constraints in accounting.

CONSTRAINTS IN ACCOUNTING

◆ Constraints permit a company to modify generally accepted accounting principles without reducing the usefulness of the reported information.

◆ The constraints are materiality and conservatism.

  1 Materiality relates to an item's impact on a firm's overall financial condition and operations.

  2 Conservatism in accounting means that, when in doubt, the accountant chooses the method that will be the least likely to overstate assets and income.

ILLUSTRATION 12-11 BASIC PRINCIPLES USED IN ACCOUNTING

Revenue Recognition

At end of production / At time of order / At time of sale

During production / At time cash received

Revenue should be recognized in the accounting period in which it is earned (generally point of sale).

Matching

Costs — Matching — Sales Revenue

Materials

Labor

Operating Expenses

Advertising Utilities Delivery

Expenses should be matched with revenues

Cost

Assets should be recorded at cost.

Full Disclosure

* Financial Statements
* Balance Sheet
* Income Statement
* Retained Earnings Statement
* Cash Flow Statement

Circumstances and events that make a difference to financial statement users should be disclosed.

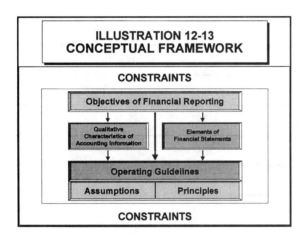

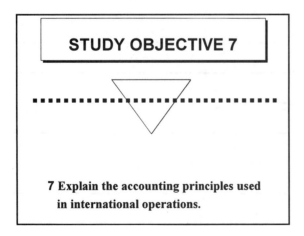

ILLUSTRATION 12-14
FOREIGN SALES AND
TYPE OF PRODUCT

World markets are becoming increasingly intertwined, and foreigners consume American goods. Americans use goods from many other countries. The table below illustrates the magnitude of foreign sales and type of products sold by U.S. companies.

Company	Foreign Sales as a % of Total	Product
Caterpillar	22.6	Heavy machinery, engines, turbines
Coca-Cola	68.3	Beverages
Eastman Kodak	52.5	Photographic equipment and supplies
E.I. duPont de Nemours	42.1	Specialty chemicals
Exxon	77.4	Petroleum, chemicals
Ford Motor	29.6	Motor vehicles and parts
General Motors	28.4	Motor vehicles and parts
Hewlett-Packard	54.1	Computers, electronics
IBM	62.3	Computers and related equipment
Philip Morris Cos.	30.4	Tobacco, beverages, food products

CHAPTER 12
ACCOUNTING PRINCIPLES

WILEY
Publishers Since 1807

Chapter 13
Accounting for Partnerships

Accounting Principles, 5e
Weygandt, Kieso, & Kimmel

Prepared by
Marianne Bradford
The University of Tennessee
Gregory K. Lowry
Mercer University

John Wiley & Sons, Inc.

CHAPTER 13
ACCOUNTING FOR PARTNERSHIPS

After studying this chapter, you should be able to:

1 Identify the characteristics of the partnership form of business organization.

2 Explain the accounting entries for the formation of a partnership.

3 Identify the bases for dividing net income or net loss.

4 Describe the form and content of partnership financial statements.

CHAPTER 13
ACCOUNTING FOR PARTNERSHIPS

After studying this chapter, you should be able to:

5 Explain the effects of the entries when a new partner is admitted.

6 Describe the effects of the entries when a partner withdraws from the firm.

7 Prepare the entries to record the liquidation of a partnership.

PREVIEW OF CHAPTER 13

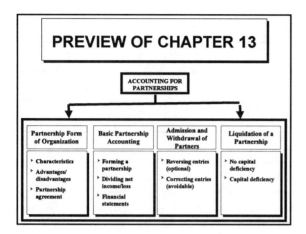

ACCOUNTING FOR PARTNERSHIPS

Partnership Form of Organization	Basic Partnership Accounting	Admission and Withdrawal of Partners	Liquidation of a Partnership
➤ Characteristics ➤ Advantages/ disadvantages ➤ Partnership agreement	➤ Forming a partnership ➤ Dividing net income/loss ➤ Financial statements	➤ Reversing entries (optional) ➤ Correcting entries (avoidable)	➤ No capital deficiency ➤ Capital deficiency

STUDY OBJECTIVE 1

1 Identify the characteristics of the partnership form of business organization.

PARTNERSHIP FORM OF ORGANIZATION

- The Uniform Partnership Act provides the basic rules for the formation and operation of partnerships in more than 90% of the states.
- The Act defines a partnership as an association of two or more persons to carry on as co-owners of a business for a profit.

CHARACTERISTICS OF PARTNERSHIPS

The principal characteristics of the partnership form of business organization are:

1 Association of individuals
2 Mutual agency
3 Limited life
4 Unlimited liability
5 Co-ownership of property

ILLUSTRATION 13-1 PARTNERSHIP CHARACTERISTICS

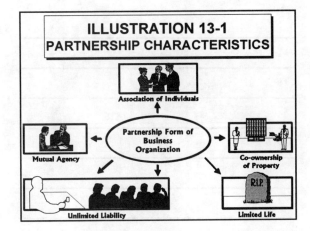

Association of Individuals

Mutual Agency

Partnership Form of Business Organization

Co-ownership of Property

Unlimited Liability

Limited Life

ASSOCIATION OF INDIVIDUALS

- The association of individuals in a partnership may be based on as simple an act as a handshake; however, it is preferable to state the agreement in writing.
- A partnership is a legal entity for certain purposes (i.e., property can be owned in the name of the partnership).
- A partnership is an accounting entity for financial reporting purposes.
- Net income of a partnership is not taxed as a separate entity; each partner's share of income is taxable at personal tax rates.

MUTUAL AGENCY

- Mutual agency means that each partner acts on behalf of the partnership when engaging in partnership business, and the act of any partner is binding on all other partners.
- The act of any partner is binding on all other partners, even when partners act beyond the scope of their authority, so long as the act appears to be appropriate for the partnership.

LIMITED LIFE

- Partnerships have a limited life.
- Partnership dissolution occurs whenever a partner withdraws or a new partner is admitted.
- Partnerships end involuntarily by death or incapacity of a partner.
- Partnerships may end voluntarily through acceptance of a new partner or withdrawal of a partner.

UNLIMITED LIABILITY

- Unlimited liability means that each partner is personally and individually liable for all partnership liabilities.
- Creditors' claims attach first to partnership assets and then to the personal resources of any partner, irrespective of that partner's capital equity in the company.
- Under limited partnerships, the liability of a limited partner is limited to the partner's capital equity; however, there must always be at least one partner with unlimited liability, often referred to as the general partner.

LIMITED PARTNERSHIPS

- Under limited partnerships, the liability of a limited partner is limited to the partner's capital equity.
- In limited partnerships, there must always be at least one partner with unlimited liability, often referred to as the general partner.

CO-OWNERSHIP OF PROPERTY

- Partnership assets are co-owned by the partners; once assets have been invested in the partnership they are owned jointly by all the partners.
- Partnership income or loss is also co-owned; if the partnership contract does not specify to the contrary, net income or net loss is shared equally by the partners.

ILLUSTRATION 13-2 ADVANTAGES AND DISADVANTAGES OF A PARTNERSHIP

Advantages	Disadvantages
Combining skills and resources of two or more individuals	Mutual agency
Ease of formation	Limited life
Freedom from governmental regulations and restrictions	Unlimited liability
Ease of decision making	

THE PARTNERSHIP AGREEMENT

- The written contract referred to as the partnership agreement (articles of co-partnership) contains such basic information as the name and principal location of the firm, the purpose of the business, and the date of inception.
- The following relationships among the partners should be specified:
  1 Names and capital contributions of the partners.
  2 Rights and duties of partners.
  3 Basis for sharing net income or net loss.
  4 Provision for withdrawals of assets.
  5 Procedures for submitting disputes to arbitration.
  6 Procedures for the withdrawal or addition of a partner.
  7 Rights and duties of surviving partners in the event of a partner's death.

STUDY OBJECTIVE 2

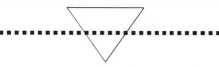

2 Explain the accounting entries for the formation of a partnership.

FORMING A PARTNERSHIP

- Each partner's initial investment in a partnership should be recorded at the fair market value of the assets at the date of their transfer to the partnership.
- The values assigned must be agreed to by all of the partners.
- After the partnership has been formed, the accounting is similar to accounting for transactions of any other type of business organization.

Upon the formation of a partnership, this personal computer should be recorded at its FMV of $2,500 instead of book value, which after depreciation may be much smaller.

ILLUSTRATION 13-6
INCOME STATEMENT WITH
DIVISION OF NET INCOME

Sara King and Ray Lee are copartners in the Kingslee Company. The partnership agreement provides for 1 salary allowances of $8,400 for Sara and $6,000 for Ray, 2 interest allowances of 10% on capital balances at the beginning of the year, and 3 the remainder equally. The division of the 1999 net income of $22,000 is as follows:

KINGSLEE COMPANY
Income Statement
For the Year Ended December 31, 1999

Sales		$ 200,000
Net income		$ 22,000

Division of Net Income

	Sara King	Ray Lee	Total
Salary allowance	$ 8,400	$ 6,000	$ 14,400
Interest allowance			
Sara King ($28,000 X 10%)	2,800		
Ray Lee ($24,000 X 10%)		2,400	
Total interest			5,200
Total salaries and interest	11,200	8,400	19,600
Remaining income – $2,400 ($22,000 – $19,600)			
Sara King ($2,400 X 50%)	1,200		
Ray Lee ($2,400 X 50%)		1,200	
Total remainder			2,400
Total division	$ 12,400	$ 9,600	$ 22,000

SALARIES, INTEREST, AND
REMAINDER ON A FIXED RATIO

Capital balances on January 1, 1999 were Sara King – $28,000 and Ray Lee – $24,000. The entry to record the division of net income is:

Date	Account Titles and Explanation	Debit	Credit
Dec. 31	Income Summary	22,000	
	Sara King, Capital		12,400
	Ray Lee, Capital		9,600
	(To close net income to partners' capitals)		

ILLUSTRATION 13-7
DIVISION OF NET INCOME
INCOME DEFICIENCY

Net income in Kingslee Company is assumed to be only $18,000. In this case, the salary and interest allowances will create a $1,600 deficiency ($19,600 – $18,000). Since the calculations of the allowances are the same as in Illustration 13-6, the division of net income will begin with total salaries and interest, as shown below.

	Sara King	Ray Lee	Total
Total salaries and interest	$ 11,200	$ 8,400	$ 19,600
Remaining deficiency – $1,600 ($18,000 – $19,600)			
Sara King ($1,600 X 50%)	(800)		
Ray Lee ($1,600 X 50%)		(800)	
Total remainder			(1,600)
Total division	$ 10,400	$ 7,600	$ 18,000

CLOSING ENTRIES

The following 4 closing entries are required for a partnership:

1 Debit each revenue account for its balance and credit Income Summary for total revenues.

2 Debit Income Summary for total expenses and credit each expense account for its balance.

3 Debit (credit) Income Summary for its balance and credit (debit) each partner's capital account for his or her share of net income (net loss).

4 Debit each partner's capital account for the balance in that partner's drawing account and each partner's drawing account for the same amount.

CLOSING ENTRIES

The first 2 entries are the same as a proprietorship, while the last 2 entries are different because:

1 there are 2 or more owners' capital and drawing accounts and

2 it is necessary to divide net income or loss among the partners.

ILLUSTRATION 13-4
CLOSING NET INCOME AND DRAWING ACCOUNTS

The AB Company has net income of $32,000 for 1999. The partners, L. Arbor and D. Barnett, share net income and net loss equally, and drawings for the year were Arbor $8,000 and Barnett $6,000. The last 2 closing entries are:

Date	Account Titles and Explanation	Debit	Credit
Dec. 31	Income Summary	32,000	
	L. Arbor, Capital ($32,000 X 50%)		16,000
	D. Barnett, Capital ($32,000 X 50%)		16,000
	(To transfer net income to owners' capital)		
31	L. Arbor, Capital	8,000	
	D. Barnett, Capital	6,000	
	L. Arbor, Drawing		8,000
	D. Barnett, Drawing		6,000
	(To close drawing accounts to capital accounts)		

ILLUSTRATION 13-5
PARTNERS' CAPITAL AND DRAWING ACCOUNTS AFTER CLOSING

Assuming the beginning capital balance is $47,000

for Arbor and $36,000 for Barnett, the capital and drawing accounts will show the following after posting the closing entries:

L. Arbor, Capital

12/31	Closing	8,000	1/1	Balance	47,000
			12/31	Closing	16,000
			12/31	Balance	55,000

L. Arbor, Drawing

12/31	Balance	8,000	12/31	Closing	8,000

D. Barnett, Capital

12/31	Closing	6,000	1/1	Balance	36,000
			12/31	Closing	16,000
			12/31	Balance	46,000

D. Barnett, Drawing

12/31	Balance	6,000	12/31	Closing	6,000

STUDY OBJECTIVE 3

3 Identify the bases for dividing net income or net loss.

INCOME RATIOS

The partnership agreement should specify the basis for sharing net income or net loss, and the following are typical of the ratios that may be used:

1 A fixed ratio, expressed as a proportion (6:4), a percentage (60% and 40%), or a fraction (3/5 and 2/5).

2 A ratio based on either capital balances at the beginning of the year or on average capital balances during the year.

3 Salaries to partners and the remainder on a fixed ratio.

4 Interest on partners' capitals and the remainder on a fixed ratio.

5 Salaries to partners, interest on partners' capitals, and the remainder on a fixed ratio.

TYPICAL INCOME-SHARING RATIOS FIXED RATIO

If A. Hughes and D. Lane are partners, each contributing the same amount of capital, but Hughes expects to work full-time and Lane only part-time, a 2/3, 1/3 fixed ratio may be equitable. The entry to close $21,000 net income to partner's capital accounts is:

Date	Account Titles and Explanation	Debit	Credit
Dec. 31	Income Summary	21,000	
	A. Hughes, Capital ($21,000 X 2/3)		14,000
	D. Lane, Capital ($21,000 X 1/3)		7,000
	(To transfer net income to owners' capital accounts)		

TYPICAL INCOME-SHARING RATIOS – CAPITAL BALANCES

- This income-sharing ratio may be based either on capital balances at the beginning of the year or on average capital balances during the year.
- Capital balances income-sharing may be equitable when a manager is hired to run the business, and the partners do not plan to take an active role in daily operations.

TYPICAL INCOME-SHARING RATIOS – SALARIES

- Income-sharing based on salary allowances may be:
  1 Salary allowances to partners and the remainder on a fixed ratio or
  2 Salary allowances to partners, interest on partners' capitals, and the remainder on a fixed ratio.
- Salaries to partners and interest on partner's capital balances are not expenses of the partnership; therefore, these items do not enter into the matching of expense with revenues and the determination of net income or net loss.

ILLUSTRATION 13-3
BOOK AND MARKET VALUE OF ASSETS INVESTED

A. Rolfe and T. Shea combine their proprietorships to start a partnership. They have the following assets prior to the formation of the partnership:

	Book Value		Market Value	
	A. Rolfe	T. Shea	A. Rolfe	T. Shea
Cash	$ 8,000	$ 9,000	$ 8,000	$ 9,000
Office equipment	5,000		4,000	
Accumulated depreciation	(2,000)			
Accounts receivable		4,000		4,000
Allowance for doubtful accounts		(700)		(1,000)
	$ 11,000	$ 12,300	$ 12,000	$ 12,000

RECORDING INVESTMENTS IN A PARTNERSHIP

Entries to record the investments are:

Account Titles and Explanation	Debit	Credit
Investment of A. Rolfe		
Cash	8,000	
Office Equipment	4,000	
A. Rolfe, Capital		12,000
(To record investment of Rolfe)		
Investment of T. Shea		
Cash	9,000	
Accounts Receivable	4,000	
Allowance for Doubtful Accounts		1,000
T. Shea, Capital		12,000
(To record investment of Shea)		

DIVIDING NET INCOME OR NET LOSS

- Partnership net income or net loss is shared equally unless the partnership contract specifically indicates otherwise.

- The same basis of division usually applies to both net income and net loss, and is called the income ratio, or the profit and loss ratio.

- A partner's share of net income or net loss is recognized in the accounts through closing entries.

STUDY OBJECTIVE 4

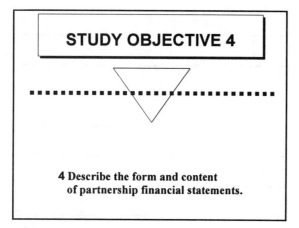

4 Describe the form and content
of partnership financial statements.

ILLUSTRATION 13-8
PARTNER'S CAPITAL STATEMENT

The owners' equity statement for a partnership is called the partners' capital statement. Its function is to explain the changes 1 in each partner's capital account and 2 in

KINGSLEE COMPANY
Partners' Capital Statement
For the Year Ended December 31, 1999

	Sara King	Ray Lee	Total
Capital, January 1	$ 28,000	$ 24,000	$52,000
Add: Additional investment	2,000		2,000
Net income	12,400	9,600	22,000
	42,400	33,600	76,000
Less: Drawings	7,000	5,000	12,000
Capital, December 31	$ 35,400	$ 28,600	$ 64,000

total partnership capital during the year. The enclosed partners' capital statement for the Kingslee Company is based on the division of $22,000 of net income in Illustration 13-6.

ILLUSTRATION 13-9
OWNER'S EQUITY SECTION OF A
PARTNERSHIP BALANCE SHEET

The partners' capital statement is prepared from the income statement and the partners' capital and drawing accounts. The balance sheet for

KINGSLEE COMPANY
Balance Sheet - partial
December 31, 1999

Total liabilities (assumed amount)		$ 115,000
Owners' equity		
Sara King, Capital	$ 35,400	
Ray Lee, Capital	28,600	
Total owners' equity		64,000
Total liabilities and owners' equity		$ 179,000

a partnership is the same as for a proprietorship except in the owners' equity section. The capital balances of the partners are shown in the balance sheet. The owners' equity section of the balance sheet for Kingslee Company is enclosed.

STUDY OBJECTIVE 5

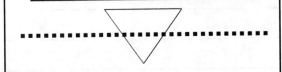

5 Explain the effects of the entries when a new partner is admitted.

ADMISSION OF A PARTNER

- The admission of a new partner results in the legal dissolution of the existing partnership and the beginning of a new partnership.
- To recognize economic effects, it is necessary only to open a capital account for each new partner.
- A new partner may be admitted either by:
  1 Purchasing the interest of one or more existing partners or
  2 Investing assets in a partnership.

ILLUSTRATION 13-10
PROCEDURES IN ADDING PARTNERS

Admission of Partner through:

I. Purchase of a Partner's Interest

The admission of a partner by purchase of an interest in the firm is a personal transaction between one or more existing partners and the new partner. The price paid is negotiated and determined by the individuals involved; it may be equal to or different from the capital equity acquired. Any money or other consideration exchanged is the personal property of the participants and not the property of the partnership.

ILLUSTRATION 13-10
PROCEDURES IN ADDING PARTNERS

When a partner is admitted by investment, both the total net assets and the total partnership capital change. When the new partner's investment differs from the capital equity acquired, the difference is considered a bonus either to: 1 The existing (old) partners or 2 The new partner.

II. Investment of Assets in Partnership

ILLUSTRATION 13-11
LEDGER BALANCES AFTER PURCHASE OF A PARTNER'S INTEREST

L. Carson agrees to pay $10,000 each to to C. Ames and D. Barker for 1/3 of their interest in the Ames-Barker partnership. At the time of the admission of Carson, each partner has a $30,000 capital balance. Both partners therefore give up $10,000 of their capital equity. The entry to record the admission of Carson is shown.

Account Titles and Explanation	Debit	Credit
C. Ames, Capital	10,000	
D. Barker, Capital	10,000	
L. Carson, Capital		20,000
(To record admission of Carson by purchase)		

Net Assets		C. Ames, Capital	
60,000		10,000	30,000
		Balance	20,000

D. Barker, Capital		L. Carson, Capital	
10,000	30,000		20,000
Balance	20,000		

ILLUSTRATION 13-12
LEDGER BALANCES AFTER INVESTMENT OF ASSETS

Assume that instead of purchasing an interest, Carson invests $30,000 in cash in the Ames-Barker partnership for a 1/3 capital interest. In such a case, the entry would be as shown. The effects of this transaction on the partnership accounts are shown in the t-accounts.

Account Titles and Explanation	Debit	Credit
Cash	30,000	
L. Carson, Capital		30,000
(To record admission of Carson by investment)		

Net Assets		C. Ames, Capital	
60,000			30,000
30,000			
Balance	90,000		

D. Barker, Capital		L. Carson, Capital	
	30,000		30,000

ILLUSTRATION 13-13
COMPARISON OF PURCHASE OF AN INTEREST AND ADMISSION BY INVESTMENT

The different effects of the purchase of an interest and admission by investment are shown in the comparison of net assets and capital balances. When an interest is purchased, the total net assets and total capital of the partnership do not change. On the other hand, when a partner is admitted by investment, both the total net assets and the total capital change. For an admission by investment, when the new partner's investment and the capital equity acquired are different, the difference is considered a bonus to either

1 the old partners or

2 the new partner.

	Purchase of an Interest	Admission by Investment
Net Assets	$ 60,000	$ 90,000
Capital		
C. Ames	$ 20,000	$ 30,000
D. Barker	20,000	30,000
L. Carson	20,000	30,000
Total capital	$ 60,000	$ 90,000

BONUS TO OLD PARTNERS

A bonus to old partners results when the new partner's capital credit on the date of admittance is less than the new partner's investment in the firm. The procedure for determining the new partner's capital credit and the bonus to the old partners is as follows:

1 Determine the total capital of the new partnership by adding the new partner's investment to the total capital of the old partnership.

2 Determine the new partner's capital credit by multiplying the total capital of the new partnership by the new partner's ownership interest.

3 Determine the amount of bonus by subtracting the new partner's capital credit from the new partner's investment.

4 Allocate the bonus to the old partners on the basis of their income ratios.

BONUS TO OLD PARTNERS

The Bart-Cohen partnership owned by Sam Bart and Tom Cohen has total capital of $120,000 when Lea Eden is admitted to the partnership. Lea acquires a 25% ownership interest by making a cash investment of $80,000 in the partnership. The procedure for determining Eden's capital credit and the bonus to the old partners is as follows:

1. Determine the total capital of the new partnership by adding the new partner's investment to the total capital of the old partnership. In this case, the total capital of the new firm is $200,000, calculated as follows:

Total capital of existing partnership	$ 120,000
Investment by new partner, Eden	80,000
Total capital of new partnership	$ 200,000

2. Determine the new partner's capital credit by multiplying the total capital of the new partnership by the new partner's ownership interest. Eden's capital credit is $50,000 ($200,000 X 25%).

BONUS TO OLD PARTNERS

3. **Determine the amount of bonus** by subtracting the new partner's capital credit from the new partner's investment. The bonus in this case is $30,000 ($80,000 – $50,000).

4. **Allocate the bonus to the old partners** on the basis of their income ratios. Assuming the ratios are Bart, 60% and Cohen, 40%, the allocation is: Bart, $18,000 ($30,000 X 60%) and Cohen, $12,000 ($30,000 X 40%). The entry to record the admission is:

Account Titles and Explanation	Debit	Credit
Cash	80,000	
Sam Bart, Capital		18,000
Tom Cohen, Capital		12,000
Lea Eden, Capital		50,000
(To record admission of Eden and bonus to old partners)		

BONUS TO NEW PARTNER

- A bonus to a new partner results when the new partner's capital credit is greater than the partner's investment of assets in the firm.
- The capital balances of the old partners are decreased based on their income ratios before the admission of the new partner.

 — BONUS

ILLUSTRATION 13-14
COMPUTATION OF CAPITAL CREDIT AND BONUS TO NEW PARTNER

Lea Eden invests $20,000 in cash for a 25% ownership interest in the Bart-Cohen partnership. The calculations for Eden's capital credit and the bonus are as follows:

1. Total capital of Bart-Cohen partnership	$ 120,000	3. Bonus to Eden ($35,000 – $20,000)		$ 15,000
Investment by new partner, Eden	20,000			
Total capital of new partnership	$ 140,000	4. Allocation of bonus:		
		Bart ($15,000 X 60%)		$ 9,000
2. Eden's capital credit (25% X $140,000)	$ 35,000	Cohen ($15,000 X 40%)		6,000
				$ 15,000

The entry to record the admission of Eden is as follows:

Account Titles and Explanation	Debit	Credit
Cash	20,000	
Sam Bart, Capital	9,000	
Tom Cohen, Capital	6,000	
Lea Eden, Capital		35,000
(To record Eden's admission and bonus)		

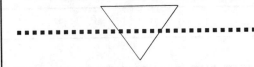

STUDY OBJECTIVE 6

6 Describe the effects of the entries when a partner withdraws from the firm.

_____

_____

_____

_____

_____

_____

WITHDRAWAL OF A PARTNER

● A partner may withdraw from a partnership voluntarily by selling his or her equity in the firm or involuntarily by reaching mandatory retirement age or by dying.

● The withdrawal of a partner may be accomplished by

1 payment from remaining partners' personal assets or

2 payment from partnership assets.

_____

_____

_____

_____

_____

_____

ILLUSTRATION 13-15 PROCEDURES IN PARTNERSHIP WITHDRAWAL

Withdrawal of Partner through:

I. Payment from Partners' Personal Assets

II. Payment from Partnership Assets

_____

_____

_____

_____

_____

_____

PAYMENT FROM PARTNERS' PERSONAL ASSETS

- The withdrawal of a partner when payment is made from partners' personal assets is the direct opposite of admitting a new partner who purchases a partner's interest.
- Withdrawal by payment from partners' personal assets is a personal transaction between the partners.

ILLUSTRATION 13-16
LEDGER BALANCES AFTER PAYMENT FROM PARTNERS' PERSONAL ASSETS

Anne Morz, Mary Nead, and Jill Odom have capital balances of $25,000, $15,000, and $10,000, respectively, when Morz and Nead agree to buy out Odom's interest. Each of them agrees to pay Odom $8,000 in exchange for one-half of Odom's total interest of $10,000. The entry to record the withdrawal is:

Account Titles and Explanation	Debit	Credit
Jill Odom, Capital	10,000	
Anne Morz, Capital		5,000
Mary Nead, Capital		5,000
(To record purchase of Odom's Interest)		

The effect of this entry on the partnership accounts is shown below:

Net Assets		Anne Morz, Capital		Mary Nead, Capital		Jill Odom, Capital	
50,000			25,000		15,000	10,000	10,000
			5,000		5,000		
		Bal.	30,000	Bal.	20,000	Bal.	-0-

PAYMENT FROM PARTNERSHIP ASSETS

Using partnership assets to pay for a withdrawing partner's interest decreases both total assets and total partnership capital. In accounting for a withdrawal by payment from partnership assets:

1 asset revaluations should not be recorded and

2 any difference between the amount paid and the withdrawing partner's capital balance should be considered a bonus to the retiring partner or a bonus to the remaining partners.

BONUS TO RETIRING PARTNER

A bonus may be paid to a retiring partner when:

1 the fair market value of partnership assets is greater than their book value,

2 there is unrecorded goodwill resulting from the partnership's superior earnings record, or

3 the remaining partners are anxious to remove the partner from the firm.

BONUS

BONUS TO RETIRING PARTNER

The bonus is deducted from the remaining partners' capital balances on the basis of their income ratios at the time of the withdrawal. Terk retires from the RST partnership and receives a cash payment of $25,000 from the firm. The procedure for determining the bonus to the retiring partner and the allocation of the bonus to the remaining partners is: 1 Determine the amount of the bonus by subtracting the retiring partner's capital balance from the cash paid by the partnership. The bonus in this case is $5,000 ($25,000 – $20,000). 2 Allocate the bonus to the remaining partners on the basis of their income ratios. The ratios of Roman and Sand are 3:2, so the allocation of the $5,000 bonus is: Roman $3,000 ($5,000 X 3/5) and Sand $2,000 ($5,000 X 2/5). The appropriate entry is:

Account Titles and Explanation	Debit	Credit
Betty Terk, Capital	20,000	
Fred Roman, Capital	3,000	
Dee Sand, Capital	2,000	
Cash		25,000
(To record withdrawal of and bonus to Terk)		

BONUS TO REMAINING PARTNERS

The retiring partner may pay a bonus to the remaining partners when:

1 recorded assets are overvalued,

2 the partnership has a poor earnings record, or

3 the partner is anxious to leave the partnership.

BONUS

BONUS TO REMAINING PARTNERS

The bonus is allocated (credited) to the capital balances of the remaining partners on the basis of their income ratios. Assume that Terk is paid only $16,000 for her $20,000 equity upon withdrawing from the RST partnership. In such a case: 1 The bonus to remaining partners is $4,000 ($20,000 – $16,000). 2 The allocation of the $4,000 bonus is: Roman $2,400 ($4,000 X 3/5) and Sand $1,600 ($4,000 X 2/5). The entry to record the withdrawal is:

Account Titles and Explanation	Debit	Credit
Betty Terk, Capital	20,000	
Fred Roman, Capital		2,400
Dee Sand, Capital		1,600
Cash		16,000
(To record withdrawal of Terk and bonus to remaining partners)		

DEATH OF A PARTNER

- The death of a partner dissolves the partnership, but provision generally is made for the surviving partners to continue operations by purchasing the deceased partner's equity from their personal assets.

- When a partner dies it is necessary to determine the partner's equity at the date of death. This is done by:

1 determining the net income or loss for the year to date,

2 closing the books, and

3 preparing financial statements.

DEATH OF A PARTNER

- The surviving partners will agree to either

1 purchase the deceased partner's equity from their personal assets or

2 use partnership assets to settle with the deceased partners estate.

- In both instances, the entries to record the withdrawal of the partner are similar to those in previous illustrations.

LIQUIDATION OF A PARTNERSHIP

- The liquidation of a partnership terminates the business. In a liquidation, it is necessary to:

  1 sell noncash assets for cash and recognize a gain or loss on realization,

  2 allocate gain/loss on realization to the partners based on their income ratios,

  3 pay partnership liabilities in cash, and

  4 distribute remaining cash to partners on the basis of their remaining capital balances.

- Each of the steps:

  1 must be performed in sequence because creditors must be paid before partners receive any cash distributions and

  2 must be recorded by an accounting entry.

STUDY OBJECTIVE 7

7 Prepare the entries to record the liquidation of a partnership.

ILLUSTRATION 13-17
ACCOUNT BALANCES
PRIOR TO LIQUIDATION

The term no capital deficiency means that all partners have credit balances in their capital accounts; if at least one partner's capital account has a debit balance, the situation is termed a capital deficiency. The Ace Company is liquidated when its ledger shows the following assets, liabilities, and owners' equity accounts:

Assets			Liabilities and Owners' Equity		
Cash	$	5,000	Notes payable	$	15,000
Accounts receivable		15,000	Accounts payable		16,000
Inventory		18,000	R. Arnet, Capital		15,000
Equipment		35,000	P. Carey, Capital		17,800
Accumulated depreciation – equipment	(	8,000)	W. Eaton, Capital		1,200
	$	65,000		$	65,000

LIQUIDATION OF A PARTNERSHIP
NO CAPITAL DEFICIENCY

The partners of Ace Company agree to liquidate the partnership on the following terms: 1 a cash sale of the noncash assets of the partnership to Jackson Enterprises for $75,000 and 2 payment of partnership liabilities by the partnership. The income ratios of the partners are 3:2:1, respectively. The liquidation process steps are:

1. The noncash assets (accounts receivable, inventory, and equipment) are sold for $75,000. Since the book value of these assets is $60,000 ($15,000 + $18,000 + $35,000 – $8,000), a gain of $15,000 is realized on the sale, The entry is:

Account Titles and Explanation	Debit	Credit
(1)		
Cash	75,000	
Accumulated Depreciation – Equipment	8,000	
Accounts Receivable		15,000
Inventory		18,000
Equipment		35,000
Gain on Realization		15,000
(To record realization of noncash assets)		

LIQUIDATION OF A PARTNERSHIP
NO CAPITAL DEFICIENCY

2. The gain on realization of $15,000 is allocated to the partners on their income ratios, which are 3:2:1. The entry is:

Account Titles and Explanation	Debit	Credit
(2)		
Gain on Realization	15,000	
R. Arnet, Capital ($15,000 X 3/6)		7,500
P. Carey, Capital ($15,000 X 2/6)		5,000
W. Eaton, Capital ($15,000 X 1/6)		2,500
(To allocate gain to partners' capitals)		

LIQUIDATION OF A PARTNERSHIP
NO CAPITAL DEFICIENCY

3. Partnership liabilities consist of Notes Payable $15,000 and Accounts Payable $16,000. Creditors are paid in full by a cash payment of $31,000. The entry is:

Account Titles and Explanation	Debit	Credit
(3)		
Notes Payable	15,000	
Accounts Payable	16,000	
Cash		31,000
(To record payment of partnership liabilities)		

ILLUSTRATION 13-18
LEDGER BALANCES
BEFORE DISTRIBUTION OF CASH

4. The remaining cash is distributed to the partners on the basis of their capital balances. Once the entries in the first 3 steps are posted, all partnership accounts – including Gain on Realization – will have zero balances except for 4 accounts: Cash $49,000; R. Arnet, Capital $22,500; P. Carey, Capital $22,800; and W. Eaton, Capital $3,700 – as shown below:

	Cash			R. Arnet, Capital		P. Carey, Capital		W. Eaton, Capital	
Bal.	5,000	(3) 31,000			Bal. 15,000		Bal. 17,800		Bal. 1,200
(1)	75,000				(2) 7,500		(2) 5,000		(2) 2,500
Bal.	49,000				Bal. 22,500		Bal. 22,800		Bal. 3,700

ILLUSTRATION 13-19
LEDGER BALANCES
AFTER DISTRIBUTION OF CASH

The entry to record the distribution of cash is:

Account Titles and Explanation	Debit	Credit
(4)		
R. Arnet, Capital	22,500	
P. Carey, Capital	22,800	
W. Eaton, Capital	3,700	
Cash		49,000
(To record distribution of cash to partners)		

After this entry is posted, all partnership accounts will have zero balances, as shown below:

	Cash			R. Arnet, Capital			P. Carey, Capital			W. Eaton, Capital	
Bal.	5,000	(3) 31,000	(4) 22,500	Bal. 15,000	(4) 22,800	Bal. 17,800	(4) 3,700	Bal. 1,200	
(1)	75,000	(4) 49,000		(2) 7,500		(2) 5,000		(2) 2,500	
Bal.	-0-			Bal. -0-		Bal. -0-		Bal. -0-	

LIQUIDATION OF A PARTNERSHIP
CAPITAL DEFICIENCY

A capital deficiency may be caused by 1 recurring net losses, 2 excessive drawings before liquidation, or 3 losses from realization suffered through liquidation. Ace Company is on the brink of bankruptcy. The partners decide to liquidate by having a "going-out-of-business" sale in which 1 merchandise is sold at substantial discounts and 2 the equipment is sold at auction. Cash proceeds from 1 these sales and 2 collections from customers total only $42,000. Therefore, the loss from liquidation is $18,000

($60,000 – 42,000). The steps in the liquidation process are as follows:

1. The entry for the realization of noncash assets is:

Account Titles and Explanation	Debit	Credit
(1)		
Cash	42,000	
Accumulated Depreciation – Equipment	8,000	
Loss on Realization	18,000	
Accounts Receivable		15,000
Inventory		18,000
Equipment		35,000
(To record realization of noncash assets)		

LIQUIDATION OF A PARTNERSHIP
CAPITAL DEFICIENCY

2. The loss on realization is allocated to the partners on the basis of their income ratios. The entry is:

Account Titles and Explanation	Debit	Credit
(2)		
R. Arnet, Capital ($18,000 X 3/6)	9,000	
P. Carey, Capital ($18,000 X 2/6)	6,000	
W. Eaton, Capital ($18,000 X 1/6)	3,000	
Loss on Realization		18,000
(To allocate loss on realization to partners)		

LIQUIDATION OF A PARTNERSHIP
CAPITAL DEFICIENCY

3. Partnership liabilities are paid. The entry is the same as in the previous example.

Account Titles and Explanation	Debit	Credit
(3)		
Notes Payable	15,000	
Accounts Payable	16,000	
Cash		31,000
(To record payment of partnership liabilities)		

ILLUSTRATION 13-21
LEDGER BALANCES
BEFORE DISTRIBUTION OF CASH

4. After posting the 3 entries, 2 accounts will have debit balances – Cash $16,000 and W. Eaton, Capital $1,800 – and 2 accounts will have credit balances –R. Arnet, Capital $6,000 and P. Carey, Capital $11,800, as shown below. Eaton has a capital deficiency of $1,800 and therefore owes the partnership $1,800. Arnet and Carey have a legally enforceable claim against Eaton's personal assets. The distribution of cash is still made on the basis of capital balances, but the amount will vary depending on how the deficiency is settled.

	Cash		R. Arnet, Capital		P. Carey, Capital		W. Eaton, Capital	
Bal.	5,000	(3) 31,000	(2) 9,000	Bal. 15,000	(2) 6,000	Bal. 17,800	(2) 3,000	Bal. 1,800
(1)	42,000							
Bal.	16,000			Bal. 6,000		Bal. 11,800	Bal. 1,800	

ILLUSTRATION 13-22
LEDGER BALANCES
AFTER PAYING CAPITAL DEFICIENCY

If the partner with the capital deficiency pays the amount owed the partnership, the deficiency is eliminated. If Eaton pays $1,800 to the partnership, the entry is:

Account Titles and Explanation	Debit	Credit
(a)		
Cash	1,800	
W. Eaton, Capital		1,800
(To record payment of capital deficiency by Eaton)		

	Cash			R. Arnet, Capital		P. Carey, Capital		W. Eaton, Capital	
Bal.	5,000	(3)	31,000	(2) 9,000	Bal. 15,000	(2) 6,000	Bal. 17,800	(2) 3,000	Bal. 1,200
(1)	42,000								(a) 1,800
(a)	1,800								
Bal.	17,800			Bal. 6,000		Bal. 11,800			Bal. -0-

LIQUIDATION OF A PARTNERSHIP
CAPITAL DEFICIENCY

The cash balance of $17,800 is now equal to the credit balances in the capital accounts (Arnet $6,000 + Carey $11,800), and cash is distributed on the basis of these balances. The entry (shown below) – once it is posted – will cause all accounts to have zero balances.

Account Titles and Explanation	Debit	Credit
R. Arnet, Capital	6,000	
P. Carey, Capital	11,800	
Cash		17,800
(To record distribution of cash to the partners)		

ILLUSTRATION 13-23
LEDGER BALANCES
AFTER NONPAYMENT OF CAPITAL DEFICIENCY

If a partner with a capital deficiency is unable to pay the amount owed to the partnership, the partners with credit balances must absorb the loss. The loss is allocated on the basis of the income ratios that exist between the partners with credit balances. The income ratios of Arnet and Carey are 3/5 and 2/5, respectively. The following entry is made to remove Eaton's capital deficiency.

Account Titles and Explanation	Debit	Credit
(a)		
R. Arnet, Capital ($1,800 X 3/5)	1,080	
P. Carey, Capital ($1,800 X 2/5)	720	
W. Eaton, Capital		1,800
(To record write-off of capital deficiency)		

After posting this entry, the cash and capital accounts will have the following balances:

	Cash			R. Arnet, Capital		P. Carey, Capital		W. Eaton, Capital	
Bal.	5,000	(3)	31,000	(2) 9,000	Bal. 15,000	(2) 6,000	Bal. 17,800	(2) 3,000	Bal. 1,200
(1)	42,000			(a) 1,080		(a) 720			
Bal.	16,000			Bal. 4,920		Bal. 11,080			Bal. -0-

LIQUIDATION OF A PARTNERSHIP
CAPITAL DEFICIENCY

The cash balance of $16,000 now equals the credit balances in the capital accounts (Arnet $4,920 + Carey $11,080). The entry (shown below) – once it is posted – will cause all accounts to have zero balances.

Account Titles and Explanation	Debit	Credit
R. Arnet, Capital		
P. Carey, Capital	4,920	
Cash	11,080	
(To record distribution of cash to the partners)		16,000

CHAPTER 13
ACCOUNTING FOR PARTNERSHIPS

WILEY
Publishers Since 1807